LATIN AND AMERICAN
DANCES

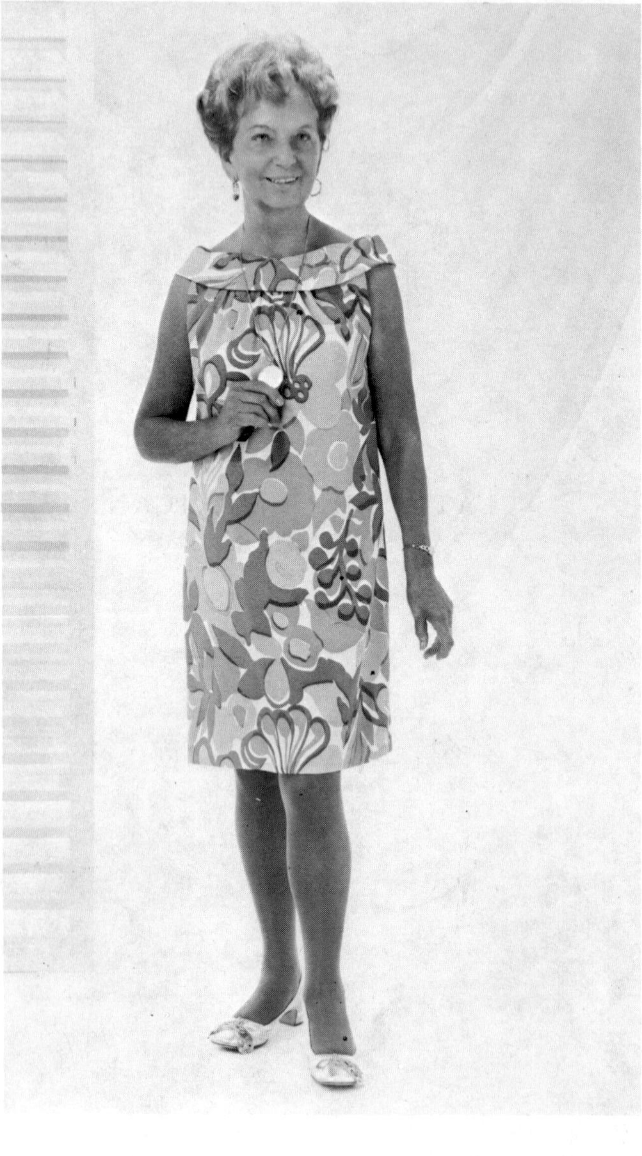

Latin and American Dances

DORIS LAVELLE

PITMAN

First published 1965
Second edition 1969
Reprinted 1970
Reprinted 1972
Revised and reprinted 1975
Reprinted 1978

PITMAN PUBLISHING LIMITED
39 Parker Street, London WC2B 5PB

Associated Companies
Copp Clark Ltd, Toronto . Fearon-Pitman Publishers Inc, Belmont, California . Pitman Publishing New Zealand Ltd, Wellington
Pitman Publishing Pty Ltd, Melbourne

©
Doris Lavelle
1965, 1969, 1975

ISBN: 0 273 41640 5

All rights reserved. No part of this publication may be reproduced, stored in a retrieval system, or transmitted, in any form or by any means, electronic, mechanical, photocopying, recording and/or otherwise, without the prior permission of the publishers. This book is sold subject to the Standard Conditions of Sale of Net Books and may not be resold in the UK below the net price.

Text set in 10pt. Monotype Baskerville, printed by photolithography
and bound in Great Britain at The Pitman Press, Bath
G.3503:14

FOREWORD

May I first say how proud I am to have been asked to write the foreword to this very important book—particularly because this request seems to indicate that I myself have met with the approval of the leading authorities in this field, who for many years have been teaching its technique in studios all over Britain!

I have had the pleasure of knowing Miss Doris Lavelle and her late partner, Monsieur Pierre, throughout the twenty-five years of the existence of my orchestra and, although we have had our differences, basically we have striven towards an identical objective—that of imparting to everyone the pleasures of Latin-American music and dancing. Many people find it difficult to put one foot before the other, much less dance well. This is why Miss Lavelle has taken such pains to explain the Rumba, Samba, Paso Doble, Cha Cha Cha, and Jive, and I believe that with the aid of the instructions and explanations she gives any child would soon be able to learn to enjoy Latin-American dancing. I sincerely look forward to seeing perform in public some of those who will have learnt their Latin-American dancing from this book.

Miss Lavelle deserves every possible success with it and I am only sorry that it was not published years ago when Monsieur Pierre—the man we regarded as the Emperor of Latin-American music and dancing in this country—could have lived to share its success. I know these must be Miss Lavelle's sentiments and I beg the reader to regard this book not only as the authentic guide to dancing the Latin-American way but as a dedication to Monsieur Pierre.   Edmundo Ros

PREFACE

INTEREST in the Latin and American Dances has steadily increased in popularity all over the world during the last fifteen years. All the important Dancing Societies in Great Britain now have a Latin and American Branch and these dances have become a serious rival to the four standard dances: Waltz, Foxtrot, Tango and Quickstep.

It was fifteen years ago that my late partner, Monsieur Pierre, first went to Cuba to study the Rumba and three years later I accompanied him to Cuba, Brazil, and North America to make an intensive study of the Rumba, Samba, American Swing—or Jive—and the Cha Cha Cha. We visited these countries regularly until Monsieur Pierre's death in 1963, and we brought back from each visit many films we had taken of expert dancers.

This book is the fruit of our long and intensive study of these dances and is intended to help the student and teacher to master the technique, and also to make it easier for the beginner to learn the simple movements. This can easily be done from the written descriptions and with the aid of the amalgamations of the basic figures to be found at the end of each dance.

Section VI, which has been added to the second edition, contains a description of certain standardized variations which are now included in the syllabus of many Dancing Societies. They will be very easily learnt once the reader has mastered the Basic Movements and Variations described in sections I to V.

D. L.

CONTENTS

Foreword by Edmundo Ros v

Preface vii

List of Figures

This is a complete list of the syllabus figures for the examination of the Imperial Society of Teachers of Dancing. The descriptions and technique of the syllabus figures have been scrutinized and approved by the Latin American Dance Branch Committee of the Society.

RUMBA

Student

	Page
Basic Movement	3–4
Fan	9
Alemana	10
Hockey Stick	12
Progressive Walks (Forward and Back)	5
Natural Top	6
Natural Opening Out Movement	7
Side Step	11
Closed Hip Twist	8
Cucarachas	12
Hand to Hand	167
Spot Turn (as steps 7, 8 and 9 of Aida)	168

Associate

	Page
Reverse Top	14
Opening Out from Reverse Top	17
Aida	168
Spiral	20
Open Hip Twist	18

Member and Fellow

	Page
Alternative Basic Movement	5
Kiki Walks	170
Sliding Doors	21
Fencing	169

	Page
Rope Spinning	24
Three Threes	25
Advanced Hip Twists	31
Questions and Answers	32–7
Amalgamations of Basic Figures	26–7
Variations	28–30

SAMBA

Student

	Page
Basic Movements (Natural, Reverse and Alternative)	40–1
Progressive Basic Movement	42
Outside Basic Movement	41
Whisks to R and L	45
Samba Walk in PP	45
Travelling Bota Fogo	55
Bota Fogo in PP and CPP	50
Reverse Turn	52
Corta Jaca	46

Associate

	Page
Closed Rocks	49
Side Samba Walk	53
Travelling Volta	176

ix

CONTENTS

Associate (*cont.*)

	Page
Shadow Bota Fogo	175
Argentine Crosses	179

Member and Fellow

Stationary Samba Walks	53
Open Rocks	58
Back Rocks	55
Plait	61
Foot Changes	173
Contra Bota Fogo from Cum Batu	67–8
Rolling off the Arm	172
Natural Roll	64
Volta Movement	175
Questions and Answers	73–6
Amalgamations of Basic Figures	64
Variations	64–73

PASO DOBLE

Student

Sur Place	78
Basic Movement	78
Appel	83
Chassés to R and L (with or without Elevation)	79
Déplacement	80
Attack (as steps 20, 21, 22 and 23 of Syncopated Separation)	97
Separation	83
Fallaway Ending to Separation	86
The Huit (Cape)	82
Sixteen	88

Associate

Promenades	90
Grand Circle (Advanced Ending to Promenades)	91
Open Telemark	102
Ecart	94
La Passe	92

Member and Fellow

Fallaway Reverse	103

	Page
Syncopated Separation	96
Banderillas	95
Twists	99
Coup de Pique	101
Left Foot Variation	181
Fregolina (Incorporating the Farol)	182, 185
Travelling Spins from PP	104
Travelling Spins from CPP	104
Chassé Cape	103
Questions and Answers	104–7
Amalgamation	100
Variations	101

JIVE

Student

Fallaway Rock	109–110
Fallaway Throwaway	126
Link	111
Change of Places Right to Left	114
Change of Places Left to Right	115
Change of Hands Behind Back	119
American Spin	122
Walks	118
Whip	112

Associate

Whip Throwaway	127
Stop and Go	128
Windmill	131
Spanish Arms	129
Rolling off the Arm	132

Member and Fellow

Simple Spin	123
Chicken Walks	134
Curly Whip	134
Toe Heel Swivels	188
Flicks into Break	185
Questions and Answers	140–3
Amalgamation	135
Variations	136–40

CHA CHA CHA

Student

	Page
Basic Movement	145
Fan	146
Alamana	147
Hockey Stick	150
Three Cha Cha Chas	163
Natural Top	153
Natural Opening Out Movement	154
Closed Hip Twist	155
Hand to Hand	148
Sport Turns	151
Time Step	151
New York	158

Associate

Shoulder to Shoulder	156
Reverse Top	162
Opening Out from Reverse Top	162
Aida	162
Spiral	160
Open Hip Twist	158

Member and Fellow

Rope Spinning	194
Advanced Hip Twist	163
Cross Basic	156
Cuban Breaks	190
Turkish Towel	193
Sweetheart	192
Follow my Leader	190
Advanced Hip Twist	162
Questions and Answers	163–6
Amalgamation	160–1
Variations	163

ABBREVIATIONS USED

THROUGHOUT the book abbreviations are used; the meanings are as follows—

RF	Right Foot
LF	Left Foot
PP	Promenade Position
CPP	Counter Promenade Position
S	Slow
Q	Quick
L.O.D.	Line of Dance
CBM	Contrary Body Movement
SP	Shadow Position

For the Rumba, Samba, Jive and Cha Cha Cha I have used four columns—

(1) Step No., (2) Position of Feet, (3) Amount of turn, (4) Timing.

For the Paso Doble I have used five, the fifth column being for Footwork, since in this dance the footwork varies considerably. The marching steps are taken with a heel lead; the small steps, "Sur Place," etc., are ball of foot or ball heel and other movements are danced on the toes.

At the end of descriptions of the basic steps in each dance and before the descriptions of the variations, I give a short amalgamation, with suggested alignments, which should help the beginner.

SECTION I

RUMBA

THE authentic ballroom Rumba, Bolero or Son, was originally taught in this country in 1947. My late partner, Pierre, visited Havana, Cuba, and found that although we had been teaching and dancing to Cuban music for some years we were not teaching it as taught and danced in Cuba. When dancing with the Cuban girls Pierre discovered that they were not happy with the rhythm he was using and upon further study with the famous professional Pepe Rivera, realized that they danced the basic step commencing on the second beat of the bar of music. As the Rumba is usually 4/4 time, counted 1, 2, 3, 4, the first step is taken on the second beat, the second step on the third beat and the third step on the fourth beat, pausing for the first beat of the next bar of music. The tempo can be very slow, medium or very fast, but when first studying this dance it is better to use the medium tempo, 30–32 bars per minute.

On Pierre's subsequent visits to Cuba I accompanied him and the steps which now make up the professional syllabuses of all the leading societies in Great Britain are the steps which we learned mainly from Pepe Rivera.

I well remember *my* first visit to Cuba. Flying over the Atlantic for the first time, coming down to refuel at Gander, New York and Jacksonville—every moment a thrill—and at last flying over the Gulf of Mexico, seeing the bright lights of Havana and landing in the magic country of Cuba. I don't know quite what I had expected—a super Monte Carlo, Lisbon, Amsterdam, Paris, all in one parcel—Havana! Well, I was disappointed. In 1952 Havana seemed rather small, no magnificent buildings, Central Park no larger than Berkeley Square and very few flowers, but Oh! how I grew to love it, principally, I think, because of the wonderful music and the charming people.

In a very short time we were well-known figures in Havana, one Frenchman, one Englishman and an Englishwoman. We were also objects of curiosity—why should we go to their country to learn their dance which they did as naturally as walking?

There were no dancing Associations in Cuba and very few teachers, so Pierre—with my help—was responsible for naming the steps which I will be describing in this book.

At that time in Cuba there were hundreds of excellent dancers. Cubans do not learn to dance but everywhere they go they hear Cuban music. It was, then, on the radio all day long, one good band after another and most of the shops had radios always switched on. It was wonderful to see even small children, whilst waiting to be served, moving their little hips to the fascinating rhythm, all on the 2, 3, 4, 1 timing.

Nobody outside Cuba now knows if they are still dancing, although I do not think you could possibly stop a Cuban dancing. A short time ago we planned to visit Cuba, but only got as far as Miami. Luckily we found some of our Cuban friends there, and were able to continue with the study of this very fascinating dance. At that time there were 60,000 Cubans in Florida and many well-known bands, whom we had known in happier times, were amongst them.

RUMBA

Tempo. 30–32 bars per minute.

Musical Timing. 2/4 and 4/4.

Timing. 4 counts to each bar of music, counted 1, 2, 3, 4.

The Hold. The gentleman holds the lady in normal ballroom hold but with no hip contact. The weight must be slightly forward, but neither lady nor gentleman must lean forward.

Basic Movement

FORWARD HALF

Entries. Basic Movement, Progressive Walk, Reverse Top, Opening out from Natural Top, Side Steps, Cucaracha, Alemana, Hockey Stick.

Step	Feet Positions	Amount of Turn	Timing
Gentleman			
1	LF forward, leaving RF in place and raising heel of RF	Commence to turn to left	2 or Q
2	Replace weight on RF	Continue to turn to left	3 or Q
3	LF to side and slightly back	Approximately ⅛ turn to left over steps 1, 2, 3	4–1 or S

Footwork. Ball flat on each step.

Note. When describing the feet position on step 1 I have used the expression "raising the heel." When the full weight is taken on to the left foot the heel of the right foot is raised about one inch from the floor, this being quite a natural movement. The heel must never be deliberately lifted. Also throughout this dance the knees must never be braced, just a normal bending and straightening action is used.

4   LATIN AND AMERICAN DANCES

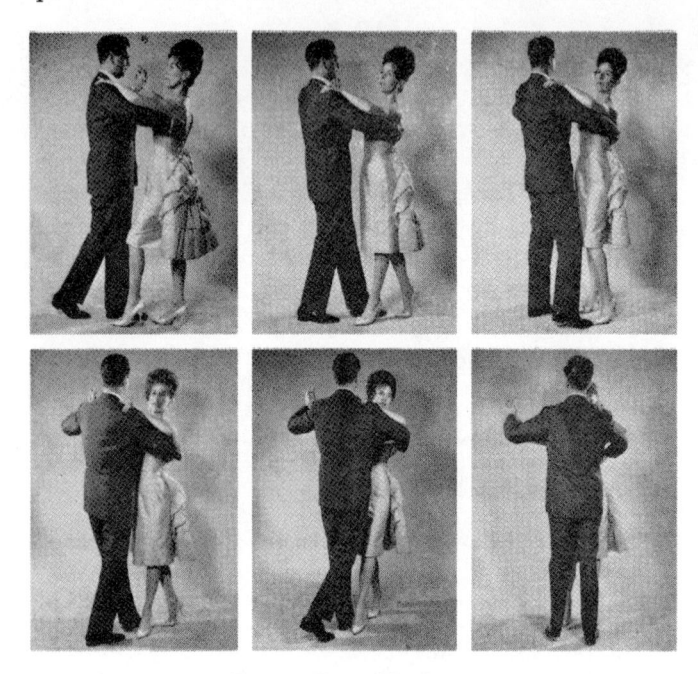

RUMBA—BASIC MOVEMENT
Forward half steps 1–3
Backward half steps 1–3

Basic Movement

BACKWARD HALF

Step	Feet Positions	Amount of Turn	Timing
Gentleman			
1	RF back, leaving LF in place, raising heel of LF	Commence to turn to left	2 or Q
2	Replace weight on LF	Continue to turn to left	3 or Q

RUMBA

3	RF to side	Approximately ⅛ turn to left over steps 1, 2, 3	4–1 or S

Footwork. Ball flat on each step.

Lady
Same steps as gentleman, opposite halves of movement.

Note. Amounts of turn can vary according to figure in which Basic Movement is used.

Exits. Basic Movement, Progressive Walk, Natural Top, Side Steps, Fan.

Alternative Basic

The alternative basic is an advanced way of dancing the forward or back Basic Movement and is used occasionally. This figure is only danced by the gentleman.

Step   *Feet Positions*   *Amount of Turn*   *Timing*

Commence with weight on RF, i.e. having opened out in Fan position.

1	Close LF to RF	None	2 or Q
2	Hesitate	None	3 or Q
3	LF to side	None	4–1 or S

This figure can also be commenced with the RF.

Footwork. Ball flat on steps 1 and 3, flat on step 2.

Progressive Walk (The Paseo)

FORWARD MOVEMENT

Entries. Basic, Reverse Top, Side Step, Cucaracha, Opening out from Natural Top, Alemana, Hockey Stick.

Note. The steps are the same for lady or gentleman.

Step	*Feet Positions*	*Amount of Turn*	*Timing*
1	LF forward relaxing left knee releasing right heel straightening left knee as weight is transferred	No turn, or curving slightly to left or right	2 or Q

Step	Feet Positions	Amount of Turn	Timing
2	Repeat with RF	—	3 or Q
3	Repeat with LF	—	4–1 or S

Footwork. Ball flat on each step.

BACKWARD

Step	Feet Positions	Amount of Turn	Timing
1	RF back relaxing right knee keeping left toe in contact with floor straightening right knee as right heel is lowered	No turn, or curving slightly to left or right	2 or Q
2	Repeat with LF	—	3 or Q
3	Repeat with RF	—	4–1 or S

Footwork. Ball flat on each step.

Exits. Basic Movement, Natural Top, Rope Spinning.

Natural Top (The Vuelta to Right)

Entries. Basic Movement, Forward Half, Progressive Walk.

Step	Feet Positions	Amount of Turn	Timing

Gentleman (after LF to side with no turn)

Step	Feet Positions	Amount of Turn	Timing
1	Place RF behind LF toe to heel	Commencing to turn to right	2 or Q
2	LF to side and slightly forward	Still turning to right	3 or Q
3	Repeat step 1	Overall amount	4–1 or S
4	Repeat step 2	of turn	2 or Q
5	Repeat step 1	approximately	3 or Q
6	Repeat step 2	1½ turns to right	4–1 or S
7	Repeat step 1	between steps	2 or Q
8	Repeat step 2	1 and 8	3 or Q
9	R closes to LF	None	4–1 or S

Footwork. Ball or ball flat on steps 1, 3, 5, 7, ball flat on steps 2, 4, 6, 8, 9.

RUMBA—NATURAL TOP
Preceding step   Steps 1, 3, 5, 7   Steps 2, 4, 6, 8

Lady (after RF forward between gentleman's feet)

1	LF to side and slightly back	Commencing to turn to right	2 or Q
2	RF placed in front of LF	Still turning to right	3 or Q
3	Repeat step 1	Overall amount	4-1 or S
4	Repeat step 2	of turn	2 or Q
5	Repeat step 1	approximately	3 or Q
6	Repeat step 2	1½ turns to right	4-1 or S
7	Repeat step 1	between steps	2 or Q
8	Repeat step 2	1 and 8	3 or Q
9	LF to side	None	4-1 or S

Footwork. Ball flat on each step.

Exits. Opening out, Rope Spinning.

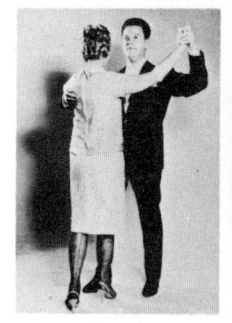

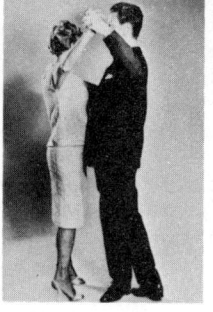

Opening Out from Natural Top

Entries. Natural Top.

Step   *Feet Positions*   *Amount of Turn*   *Timing*

Gentleman (after last step of Natural Top)

1	LF to side leaving RF in place	None	2 or Q

LATIN AND AMERICAN DANCES

Step	Feet Positions	Amount of Turn	Timing
2	Replace weight on RF leading lady to commence her turn to left	None	3 or Q
3	LF closes to RF leading lady to continue turn to normal position	None	4-1 or S

Footwork. Ball flat on each step.

Lady (after last step of Natural Top)

1	RF back and slightly to side	Approximately ½ turn to right	2 or Q
2	Replace weight forward on LF	Commence to turn to left	3 or Q
3	RF to side	Continue to turn to left, making approximately ½ turn between steps 2 and 3	4-1 or S

Footwork. Ball flat on each step.

Exits. Basic Movement, Backward Half, Reverse Top, Progressive Walk, Closed Hip Twist, Spiral.

Closed Hip Twist

Entries. Opening Out as from Natural Top.

Step	Feet Positions	Amount of Turn	Timing

Gentleman (after Opening out from Natural Top)

1	RF back	None	2 or Q
2	Replace weight forward on LF	None	3 or Q
3	RF to side	None	4-1 or S

Footwork. Ball flat on each step.

On step 1 the gentleman helps the lady by slight pressure on her waist with his right hand to swing her left hip forward and releasing her with R hand on step 2.

Note. The advanced dancer can sometimes turn a quarter to left between steps 2 and 3.

RUMBA

Step	Feet Positions	Amount of Turn	Timing
Lady (after opening out from Natural Top)			
1	LF forward	3/8 turn to right	2 or Q
2	RF back and slightly to side	5/8 turn to left between steps	3 or Q
3	LF back	2 and 3	4–1 or S

Footwork. Ball flat on each step.

On step 1 the turn must be taken on the ball of the right foot allowing the hips to turn, the shoulders being kept practically square with partner.

Exits. Alemana, Hockey Stick, Sliding Doors or, if gentleman turns, Open Hip Twist, Three Threes.

Fan (el Abanico)

Entries. Basic Movement, Forward Half, Progressive Walk.

Gentleman

Second half of Basic Movement without turning, RF, LF, RF, counted 2, 3, 4–1 or QQS, releasing hold with right hand at end of second step.

Note. The advanced dancer can turn a quarter to left between steps 2 and 3.

Rumba—The Fan
Steps 1–3

Step	Feet Positions	Amount of Turn	Timing
Lady			
1	LF forward in line with partner	No turn	2 or Q
2	RF back and slightly to side	Commence to turn to left	3 or Q
3	LF back	Continue to turn to left, making ¼ turn to left between steps 2 and 3	4–1 or S

Footwork. Ball flat on each step.

Exits. Alemana, Hockey Stick, Sliding Doors or, if the gentleman turns, Open Hip Twist, Three Threes.

Alemana (Lady's Turn to Right)

Entries. Fan, Cucaracha into last three steps of Alemana, Closed Hip Twist, Opening out from 6 of Reverse Top.

Step	Feet Positions	Amount of Turn	Timing
Gentleman			
1	LF forward	None	2 or Q
2	Replace weight on RF	None	3 or Q
3	LF closes to RF	None	4–1 or S
4	RF back	None	2 or Q
5	Replace weight on LF	None	3 or Q
6	RF closes to LF	None	4–1 or S

Footwork. Ball flat on each step.

Note. In the last three steps the gentleman lifts his left hand and holding the lady's right hand above her head leads her into a small circle to right as described below.

Step	Feet Positions	Amount of Turn	Timing
Lady			
1	RF closes to LF	None	2 or Q
2	LF forward	None	3 or Q
3	RF forward commencing to turn to right	Approximately ⅛ turn to right	4–1 or S

RUMBA

4	LF forward small step	Continue to turn to right	2 or Q
5	RF forward small step	Continue to turn to right	3 or Q
6	LF forward small step	Continue to turn to right making $1\frac{1}{8}$ turns to right between steps 4, 5, 6	4–1 or S

Footwork. Ball flat on each step.

Exits. Basic Movement, Progressive Walk.

Note. The lady when dancing the Alemana can overturn steps 4, 5, 6, to make an overall amount of turn of one and a half turns to right. On step 6 she would place her left hand on the gentleman's right shoulder and finish with the Opening out and Closed Hip Twist. She could also make an overall amount of turn of one and three-quarter turns to right to finish facing the same way as her partner and then would finish with the Opening out and Spiral.

Side Step (El Paso Lateral)

Entries. Basic Movement.

Step	Feet Positions	Amount of Turn	Timing
Gentleman (from backward half of Basic Movement)			
1	RF forward and slightly to side (3rd step of 2nd half of Basic Movement)	None	4 or Q
2	LF "brushes" to RF without weight	None	1 or Q
3	LF to side	None	2 or Q
4	RF closes to LF	None	3 or Q
5	Repeat step 3	None	4–1 or S
6	Repeat step 4	None	2 or Q
7	Repeat step 3	None	3 or Q
8	Repeat step 4	None	4–1 or S

Lady

Normal opposite.

Footwork. Ball flat on each step with the exception of step 2.

Exits. Basic Movement, Cucaracha, Progressive Walk.

Cucarachas (Pressure Steps)

Entry. Side Step.

Step	Feet Positions	Amount of Turn	Timing
Gentleman			
1	LF to side, with part weight	None	2 or Q
2	Replace full weight on RF	None	3 or Q
3	LF closes to RF	None	4–1 or S

Can also be danced commencing with RF to side.

Footwork. Ball flat on steps 1 and 3 and flat on step 2.

Lady

Normal opposite.

Exits. Basic Movement, last three steps of Alemana.

Hockey Stick (Lady's Turn to Left)

Entries. Fan, Closed Hip Twist, Opening out from 6 of Reverse Top.

Step	Feet Positions	Amount of Turn	Timing
Gentleman			
1	LF forward	None	2 or Q
2	Replace weight on RF	None	3 or Q
3	LF closes to RF	None	4–1 or S
4	RF back, short step	Body turns slightly to R	2 or Q

RUMBA 13

RUMBA—HOCKEY STICK
Steps 1, 2, 3
Steps 4, 5, 6

| 5 | Replace weight on LF | Continue to turn to R, making $\frac{1}{8}$ turn between steps 4 and 5 | 3 or Q |
| 6 | RF forward | None | 4–1 or S |

In steps 3 and 4 the gentleman lifts his left hand and holding the lady's right hand above her head, leads her to turn left.

Footwork. Ball flat on each step.

Step	Feet Positions	Amount of Turn	Timing
Lady			
1	RF closes to LF	None	2 or Q
2	LF forward	None	3 or Q
3	RF forward	None	4–1 or S
4	LF forward	Commence to turn to left making approximately $\frac{1}{8}$ turn	2 or Q
5	RF back and slightly to side	Continue turning to left making approximately $\frac{3}{8}$ turn	3 or Q
6	LF back	Continue turning to left making approximately $\frac{1}{8}$ turn	4–1 or S

Footwork. Ball flat on each step.

Exits. Basic Movement, Progressive Walk, Open Hip Twist, Three Threes.

The Reverse Top (The Vuelta to Left)

Entries. Opening out from Natural Top.

Step	Feet Positions	Amount of Turn	Timing

Gentleman (following Opening out from Natural Top on step 3 the LF is placed in front of RF, heel to toe, commencing to turn to left)

1	RF to side and slightly forward	Commencing to turn to left	2 or Q
2	LF turns on ball of foot ending with left heel to right toe	Still turning to left	3 or Q
3	Repeat step 1	Overall amount of turn approximately $1\frac{1}{2}$ turns to left between steps 1 and 9	4–1 or S
4	Repeat step 2		2 or Q
5	Repeat step 1		3 or Q
6	Repeat step 2		4–1 or S
7	Repeat step 1		2 or Q

RUMBA—REVERSE TOP
Entry into Reverse Top, showing third step of opening out

| 8 | Repeat step 2 | — | 3 or Q |
| 9 | Repeat step 1 | — | 4–1 or S |

Footwork. Ball flat on each step.

Lady (after stepping RF back and slightly to side, turning body to left on third step of Opening out from Natural Top)

1	LF crosses behind RF toe to heel	Commencing to turn to left	2 or Q
2	RF back and slightly to side	Still turning to left	3 or Q
3	Repeat step 1	Overall amount	4–1 or S
4	Repeat step 2	of turn	2 or Q
5	Repeat step 1	approximately	3 or Q
6	Repeat step 2	1½ turns to left	4–1 or S
7	Repeat step 1	between steps 1 and 9	2 or Q

RUMBA—REVERSE TOP
Steps 1, 3, 5, 7, 9   Steps 2, 4, 6, 8

Step	Feet Positions	Amount of Turn	Timing
8	Repeat step 2	—	3 or Q
9	Repeat step 1	—	4–1 or S

Footwork. Ball flat on each step.

Exits. Basic Movement, Progressive Walk, Opening out after six steps of Reverse Top.

A popular and simple finish to the Reverse Top is described below.

The Outside Swivel

Entry. Nine steps of Reverse Top.

Step	Feet Positions	Amount of Turn	Timing
Gentleman			
1	LF forward leaving RF in place	None	2 or Q

RUMBA

2	Replace weight on RF	None	3 or Q
3	LF back	None	4–1 or S
4	RF back leaving LF in place	None	2 or Q
5	Replace weight on LF	None	3 or Q
6	RF to side	None	4–1 or S

Footwork. Ball flat on each step.

Lady

1	RF back leaving LF in place	None	2 or Q
2	Replace weight on LF	None	3 or Q
3	RF forward on gentleman's right side	None	4 or Q
	Swivel	¼ turn to right	1 or Q
4	LF forward	None	2 or Q
5	RF back and slightly to side	Commence to turn to left	3 or Q
6	LF back	Continue to turn to left making ½ turn between steps 5 and 6	4–1 or S

Footwork. Ball flat on each step.

Exits. Hockey Stick, Alemana, Sliding Doors.

Opening Out from Reverse Top

Entries. Six steps of Reverse Top.

Step	*Feet Positions*	*Amount of Turn*	*Timing*
Gentleman			
1	RF to side and slightly forward releasing hold with R hand	A slight curve is made to left on steps 1 and 2	2 or Q

Step	Feet Positions	Amount of Turn	Timing
2	LF draws towards RF, heel to instep	—	3 or Q
3	RF to side	None	4–1 or S

Note. As the gentleman dances above steps he leads the lady to open out to finish in the same position as the third step of the Fan.

Footwork. Ball flat on each step.

Lady

1	LF back	A slight curve is made to left on steps 1 and 2	2 or Q
2	RF back	—	3 or Q
3	LF back	None	4–1 or S

Footwork. Ball flat on each step.

Exits. As from Fan.

Open Hip Twist

Entries. Fan, Closed Hip Twist, Open Hip Twist, Spiral, Hockey Stick, Opening out from Reverse Top.

Step	Feet Positions	Amount of Turn	Timing
Gentleman			
1	LF forward leaving RF in place	None	2 or Q
2	Replace weight on RF	None	3 or Q
3	LF nearly closed to RF	None	4–1 or S
4	RF back leaving LF in place	Commence to turn slightly to left	2 or Q
5	Replace weight on LF	Continue to turn left	3 or Q

Rumba—Open
Hip Twist

Steps 1, 2

Steps 3, 4

Steps 5, 6

Step	Feet Positions	Amount of Turn	Timing
6	RF to side	Continue to turn making approximately ¼ turn to left between steps 4, 5, 6	4–1 or S

Note. The gentleman can dance steps 4, 5, 6, without turn.

Footwork. Ball flat on each step.

Lady

1	RF closes to LF	None	2 or Q
2	LF forward	None	3 or Q
3	RF forward	None	4–1 or S
4	LF forward turning on ball of RF	Approximately ⅜ turn to right	2 or Q
5	RF back and slightly to side	Approximately ½ turn to left	3 or Q
6	LF back	Approximately ⅛ turn to left	4–1 or S

At the end of step 3 the lady braces her right arm leaning slightly on her partner's left arm, then she turns on step 4 with a strong "left hip" lead, the shoulders remaining square to partner.

Footwork. Ball flat on each step.

Exits. Open Hip Twist and Three Threes or Natural Top after both lady and gentleman have danced steps 1, 2, 3, or Alemana, Hockey Stick, and Sliding Doors if gentleman does not turn on steps 4, 5, 6.

The Spiral

Entries. Opening out as from Natural Top, six steps of Reverse Top, Sliding Doors.

Step	Feet Positions	Amount of Turn	Timing

Gentleman (after two steps of opening out from Natural Top, count 1, 2)

3	LF closes to RF	None	4–1 or S

RUMBA

4	RF back leaving LF in place	None	2 or Q
5	Replace weight on LF	Commence to turn to left	3 or Q
6	RF to side and very slightly forward	Continue to turn to left making approximately ⅛ turn between steps 5 and 6	4–1 or S

On step 3 the gentleman lifts the lady's right hand with his left hand over her head, leading her to turn to left, releasing hold with right hand on step 4.

Footwork. Ball flat on each step.

Lady (after two steps of opening out from Natural Top, count 1, 2)

3	RF to side facing partner at commencement of step	½ turn to left	4 or Q
	Turn on ball of right foot with knees locked	½ turn to left	1 or Q
4	LF forward	⅛ turn to left	2 or Q
5	RF back and slightly to side	½ turn to left between steps 5 and 6	3 or Q
6	LF back		4–1 or S

Footwork. Ball flat on each step.

Exits. Open Hip Twist, Three Threes, or steps 1, 2, 3 or Alemana into Natural Top.

Sliding Doors

Entries. Fan, Hip Twist, Open Hip Twist, Spiral, Opening out from Reverse Top.

Gentleman commences in Fan position, the lady stands on her partner's left, slightly in front of him, facing at a right angle. Only the gentleman's left hand holds the lady's right hand having released her with his right hand.

22   LATIN AND AMERICAN DANCES

Step	Feet Positions	Amount of Turn	Timing
1	LF forward leaving RF in place	None	2 or Q
2	Replace weight on RF	None	3 or Q
3	LF closes to RF	None	4–1 or S
4	RF back leaving LF in place	None	2 or Q
5	Replace weight on LF	None	3 or Q
6	RF closes to LF	None	4–1 or S
7	LF to side part weight	None	2 or Q
8	Replace weight on RF	None	3 or Q
9	LF closes to RF	None	4–1 or S
10	RF to side, part weight	None	2 or Q
11	Replace weight on LF	None	3 or Q
12	RF closes to LF	None	4–1 or S
13	LF to side	None	2 or Q
14	Replace weight on RF	None	3 or Q
15	LF closes to RF	None	4–1 or S
16	RF back leaving LF in place	None	2 or Q
17	Replace weight on LF	Commence to turn to left	3 or Q
18	RF to side and slightly forward small step	Continue to turn to left making approximately $\frac{1}{8}$ turn between steps 17 and 18	4–1 or S

Footwork. Ball flat on each step except steps 8 and 11 which are flat.

Lady (commences in Fan position)
| 1 | RF closes to LF | None | 2 or Q |
| 2 | LF forward | None | 3 or Q |

RUMBA

3	RF forward	None	4–1 or S
4	LF forward	¼ turn to left between steps 4 and 5	2 or Q
5	RF side and slightly back		3 or Q
6	LF back outside partner on right side, short step	None	4–1 or S
7	RF back leaving LF in place	None	2 or Q
8	Replace weight on LF	None	3 or Q
9	RF forward and across	None	4–1 or S
10	LF to side leaving RF in place	None	2 or Q
11	Replace weight on RF	None	3 or Q
12	LF back behind RF	None	4–1 or S
13	RF back leaving LF in place	None	2 or Q
14	Replace weight on LF	Commence to turn to left	3 or Q
15	RF to side	Completing whole turn to left	4–1 or S
16	LF forward	⅛ turn to left	2 or Q
17	RF back and slightly to side	Continue to turn to left	3 or Q
18	LF back	Approximately ½ turn to left between steps 17 and 18	4–1 or S

Footwork. Ball flat on each step.

Note. The gentleman takes the lady's left hand in his right hand on step 4, which will result in a crossed arm position on steps 5 to 14.

Exits. As from Spiral.

Rope Spinning

Entries. Natural Top, Backward Progressive Walk. After the last three steps of Natural Top the gentleman raises his left hand on the last step leading the lady to turn to the right leaning slightly towards her, releasing hold with his right hand.

Step	Feet Positions	Amount of Turn	Timing
Gentleman			
1	LF to side leaving RF in place	None	2 or Q
2	Replace weight on RF	None	3 or Q
3	LF closes to RF	None	4–1 or S
4	RF back leaving LF in place	None	2 or Q
5	Replace weight on LF	None	3 or Q
6	RF closes to LF	None	4–1 or S

Footwork. Ball flat on each step.

On step 1 the gentleman leads the lady with his left hand to continue to turn to right and commence passing behind his back. On steps 2 and 3 he continues to lead the lady with his left hand behind his back. The lady should finish with her right shoulder almost in contact with the gentleman's left shoulder, his left arm should be outstretched with the lady's right arm alongside. On steps 4 and 5 the gentleman leads the lady to circle from his left side to resume normal Rumba position on step 6.

Lady. After last three steps of Natural Top, count 2, 3, 4, then on the count of 1 commence to turn right for approximately a full turn.

1	RF forward	Curving to right	2 or Q
2	LF forward	Curving to right	3 or Q
3	RF forward	Curving to right	4–1 or S
4	LF forward	Curving to right	2 or Q
5	RF forward	Curving to right	3 or Q

| 6 | LF forward | Complete nearly a full turn between steps 1 and 6 | 4–1 or S |

Footwork. Ball flat on each step.

Exit. Forward half of basic movement.

Three Threes (Penicilina)

Entries. Hockey Stick, Spiral or, if gentleman turns to face his partner, the Fan, Closed Hip Twist, Open Hip Twist.

Step	Feet Positions	Amount of Turn	Timing
Gentleman (holding the lady's right hand in his left)			
1	LF forward keeping RF in place	None	2 or Q
2	Replace weight on RF	None	3 or Q
3	LF closes to RF	None	4–1 or S
4	RF back keeping LF in place	None	2 or Q
5	Replace weight on LF	None	3 or Q
6	RF closes to LF	None	4–1 or S
7	LF forward and slightly to side keeping part weight on RF	None	2 or Q
8	Replace weight on RF	None	3 or Q
9	LF closes to RF	None	4–1 or S
10	RF back keeping LF in place	None	2 or Q
11	Replace weight on LF	None	3 or Q
12	RF to side small step	None	4–1 or S

Footwork. Ball flat on all steps except step 8 which is flat.

On step 3 the gentleman turns the lady a half turn to right releasing her with his left hand. On step 6 he places his hands on her shoulders and turns her a full turn to left. On step 9 he places his hands on her shoulders and turns her to the right for approximately half a turn, she then goes on turning to complete one and a half turns to right to finish facing the gentleman.

Step	Feet Positions	Amount of Turn	Timing
Lady			
1	RF back	None	2 or Q
2	LF forward	None	3 or Q
3	RF forward	$\frac{1}{2}$ turn to right	4–1 or S
4	Replace weight on LF	None	2 or Q
5	Replace weight on RF	None	3 or Q
6	Replace weight on LF	Whole turn to left	4–1 or S
7	RF back and slightly to side	None	2 or Q
8	Replace weight on LF	None	3 or Q
9	RF forward	Approximately $\frac{1}{2}$ turn to right	4–1 or S
10	LF forward	Continue to turn to right	2 or Q
11	RF forward	Continue to turn to right	3 or Q
12	LF forward	Continue to turn making $1\frac{1}{2}$ turns to right between steps 9 and 12	4–1 or S

Footwork. Ball flat on all steps except step 8 which is flat.

Exit. Forward half Basic Step.

Amalgamation of Basic Figures with Suggested Alignments

Gentleman
Commence backing diagonally to centre.

RUMBA

Basic Movement, (forward half) finish facing wall.
Fan, facing wall.
Alemana, facing wall.
Forward and back Basic Movement, four times, finish facing wall having made a complete turn.
Side Step, facing wall.
Side left Cucaracha, facing wall.
Side right Cucaracha, facing wall.
Forward Basic, (no turn) facing wall.
Natural Top, (9 steps) finish backing wall.
Opening Out, still backing wall.
Reverse Top, (9 steps) finish facing wall.
Forward and back Basic Movement, four times, finish facing wall.
Basic Movement, (forward half) no turn, facing wall.
Fan, facing wall.
Hockey Stick, finish backing diagonally to centre.
Repeat from beginning.

Lady

Commence facing diagonally to centre.
Basic Movement, (backward half) finish backing wall.
Fan, finish backing L.O.D.
Alemana, finish backing wall.
Backward and forward Basic Movement, four times, finish backing wall.
Side Step, backing wall.
Side right Cucaracha, backing wall.
Side left Cucaracha, backing wall.
Basic Movement, (backward half) backing wall.
Natural Top, (9 steps) finish facing wall.
Opening Out
Reverse Top, (9 steps) finish backing wall.
Backward and forward Basic Movement, four times, finish backing wall.
Basic movement, (backward half) no turn, backing wall.
Fan, finish backing L.O.D.
Hockey Stick, finish facing diagonally to centre.
Repeat from beginning.

RUMBA VARIATIONS

The following are a selection of the most attractive figures taught and danced during the last few years.

Shoulder to Shoulder Variation

Step *Feet Positions* *Amount of Turn* *Timing*

Gentleman. This figure is preceded by the Hockey Stick, but on the sixth step the gentleman takes a rather longer step than usual and finishes with his left shoulder in line with his partner's left shoulder. He continues as follows—

Step	Feet Positions	Amount of Turn	Timing
1	LF forward outside partner on her left side	None	2
2	Replace weight on RF	Commence to turn to left	3
3	LF to side, now facing partner	Continue to turn to left	4–1
4	RF forward outside partner on her right side	Continue to turn to left to complete a ¼ turn to left between steps 2 and 4	2
5	Replace weight on LF	Commence to turn to right	3
6	RF to side now facing partner	Continue to turn to right completing ⅛ turn to R	4–1
7, 8, 9	Repeat steps 1, 2, 3		2, 3, 4–1
10	RF forward	Commence to turn left under raised left arm	2
11	LF forward	Continue to turn to left	3
12	RF forward, to finish facing partner	Continue to turn left to complete a full turn between steps 10 and 12	4–1

Footwork. Ball flat on each step.

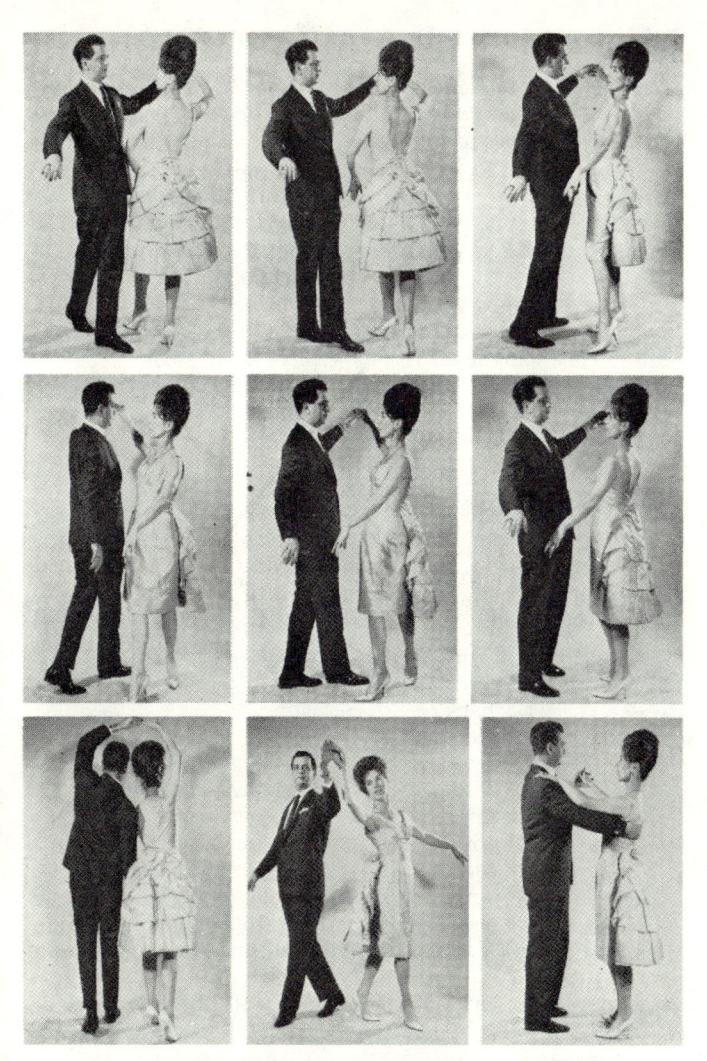

RUMBA—SHOULDER TO SHOULDER VARIATION
Steps 1 and 7, 2 and 8, 3 and 9
Steps 4, 5, 6
Steps 10, 11, 12

Step	Feet Positions	Amount of Turn	Timing

Lady. The lady dances the normal opposite on steps 1 to 9, then continues as follows—

10	LF forward	Commence to turn right under raised right arm	2
11	RF forward	Continue to turn to right	3
12	LF forward to finish facing partner	Continue to turn to right to complete a full turn between steps 10 and 12	4–1

Footwork. Ball flat on each step.

Exit. Basic Movement.

Kiki Variation

Step   Feet Positions   Amount of Turn   Timing

Gentleman. This variation is preceded by the Overturned Alemana with lady turning one and three-quarter turns to right and finishing in a position in the gentleman's right arm and both facing the same way. Gentleman continues as follows—

1	LF back	None	2
2	RF forward	Curving to left	3
3	LF forward	Curving to left	4–1
4	RF forward	Curving to left	2
5	LF forward	Curving to left	3
6	RF forward	Curving to left	4–1
7	LF forward	Curving to left	2
8	RF forward	Curving to left	3
9	LF forward	Curving to left	4–1

Finish back RF into the Fan, or on the 9th step gentleman turns ¼ turn to right and lady ¼ turn to left, or on the 9th step gentleman can turn the lady into spiral.

Lady

Dances the same steps as her partner but when he is on his RF she is on her LF and vice versa. Finish forward LF into Fan turning approximately half turn to left.

Footwork. Ball flat on each step.

Advanced Hip Twists

Step	Feet Positions	Amount of Turn	Timing

Gentleman. Commence in Closed Facing Position, RF forward, weight on RF.

1	LF forward	Slight body turn to right	2
2	Replace weight to RF	Commence to turn body to left	3
3	LF behind RF— toe to heel with toe turned out	Continue to turn left	4–1
4	RF back	Continue to turn to complete $\frac{1}{8}$ to left over steps 3 and 4	2
5	Replace weight to LF	None	3
6	RF to side and slightly forward	None	4–1

End in Fan (or Open or Close Facing) Position   <u>2 bars</u>

Lady. Commence in Closed Facing Position, feet apart, weight on LF

1	RF back	Up to $\frac{1}{2}$ turn to right	2
2	Replace weight to LF	Commence to turn left	3
3	RF forward outside partner on R side	Continue to turn to complete $\frac{5}{8}$ to left over steps 2 and 3	4–1
4	LF forward	$\frac{1}{2}$ turn to right	2
5	RF back and slightly to side	Continue to turn to complete $\frac{3}{4}$ to left over steps 5 and 6	3
6	LF back	None	4–1

End in Fan (or Open or Close Facing) Position   <u>2 bars</u>

EXAMINATION QUESTIONS AND ANSWERS

The following questions and answers are just a few of the type of questions asked in Latin and American professional examinations. Of course, the candidate would be required to demonstrate the steps as well as describe them.

Rumba for Associates

Basic Movement

Q. Describe the forward Basic Movement.

A. Forward LF raising heel of RF count 2, replace weight on RF count 3, side LF count 4–1. A slight turn of approximately one-eighth is made to left over the three steps.

Q. Is the left heel raised on the second step?

A. No, it remains flat, otherwise you would get a pedalling action.

Q. How wide should the side step be taken?

A. It depends on the size of the couple, but an average of eight to twelve inches.

Progressive Walk

Q. Are the knees bent or straight?

A. The knees should be slightly relaxed throughout the step.

Q. If curved to the right what exit could be danced?

A. Either a Basic Movement, backward half if travelling backwards or the Natural Top.

Natural Top

Q. Describe the first three steps of the Natural Top.

A. Having danced the forward half of the Basic

Movement and taken the LF slightly back, cross RF behind LF, R toe to L heel, count 2, side and slightly forward LF, count 3, cross RF behind LF toe to heel, count 4–1, making approximately half a turn to right over the three steps.

Q. On step 1 when RF crosses behind LF, does the R heel touch the floor?

A. Not necessarily, it lowers but need not touch.

Opening Out

Q. How much turn does the lady make on the first step?

A. Approximately half a turn to right.

Q. Does the gentleman dance a Cucaracha on step 1?

A. No, he steps to side with full weight on LF.

Reverse Top

Q. Describe the first three steps of Reverse Top as gentleman.

A. Having danced the Opening Out and finished with the left heel to right toe with a slight turn to left—RF to side and slightly forward, count 2, swivel on ball of LF until heel faces toe of RF, count 3, RF to side and slightly forward, count 4, 1.

Q. How much turn is made?

A. Approximately half a turn to left.

Side Step

Q. In which direction is this figure taken?

A. Usually gentleman facing wall and travelling sideways along L.O.D.

The Fan

Q. How much turn does the lady make and on which steps?

A. Quarter turn to left between steps 2 and 3.

Q. How does the gentleman lead her to open out?

A. He brings her towards him with his right hand on step 1 and gently leads her also with his right hand to move to his left side on step 2 and on step 3 she continues to move away.

Alemana

Q. How much turn does the lady make and on which steps?

A. On steps 1 and 2 no turn is made, on step 3 about one-eighth to right and between steps 4, 5, 6, she makes approximately one and one-eighth turns to right.

Q. How does the gentleman indicate that the lady is to dance the Alemana and not the Hockey Stick?

A. On the third step he leads her to move to face him, whereas in the Hockey Stick he leads her straight forward.

Hockey Stick

Q. How much turn does the lady make and why is the step called the Hockey Stick?

A. She makes five-eighths turn to left between steps 4 and 6. It is named the Hockey Stick because the first three steps represent the handle and the last three steps the curved top.

Hip Twist

Q. How much turn does the lady make?

A. Three-eighths turn to right on step 1, and five-eighths turn to left between steps 2 and 3.

Q. Why is it called a Hip Twist?

A. Because on step 1 the lady steps forward with the LF swinging her left hip forward but keeping her shoulders square with her partner.

Members' and Fellows' Syllabus

The Open Hip Twist

Q. On which count does the lady dance the hip twist?

A. On count 2.

Q. What is a common fault?

A. For the lady to commence her hip twist on the preceding count of 1.

The Spiral

Q. Give a common fault as gentleman.

A. The gentleman often steps forward on the 6th step, he should take a small step to side and only slightly forward.

Q. Give the overall amount of turn as lady.

A. Having opened out and finished facing partner, she then makes approximately one and one-eighth turn to left.

The Opening out from Reverse Top

Q. Give an exit to this figure.

A. As it finishes in Fan position, any figure that follows the Fan can be used.

Rope Spinning

Q. How does the gentleman lead his partner?

A. He gives his partner a sharp turn with his left hand on the count of 1 on the last 4–1 of the Natural Top, to enable her to turn approximately a full turn to her right, under his left and her right raised arms, he then leads her to curve to right behind his back from his right to his left side, count 2, 3, 4, 1, both arms are now outstretched and the man's left shoulder is almost in contact with the lady's right shoulder. Still leading with the left hand he leads her forward still curving to right to finish facing him, count 2, 3, 4, 1.

Q. Does the gentleman remain upright throughout the figure?

A. No, when she passes behind his back from his right side to his left side he leans slightly rightwards and slightly forward when she moves from his left side to face him. This is why it is called rope spinning.

Sliding Doors

Q. How does the gentleman indicate to the lady that she is to dance sliding doors and not continue with the Hockey Stick?

A. On the count of 4–1 of the first 2, 3, 4, 1, the gentleman has his right hand slightly forward ready to take the lady's left hand on the next count of 2.

Three Threes

Q. How much turn does the lady make?

A. Half turn to right on the first count of 4, 1; one full turn to left on the second count of 4, 1; one and a half turns to right commenced on the third count of 4, 1 and continued for the next count of 2, 3, 4, 1.

RUMBA

Q. Does the lady dance a Progressive Walk turning on the last three steps?

A. She can dance the Progressive Walk or she can dance a back Cucaracha with the LF, leaving RF in place, count 2, replace weight on RF still turning, count 3, side LF count 4, 1.

SECTION II

THE SAMBA

The following figures now form a syllabus for nearly all Dancing Societies in Great Britain and have been selected because they are the most suitable ones to dance to the speed of Samba music generally heard in this country.

When I, with Pierre, visited Rio de Janeiro in 1956 it was to see for ourselves just what the Brazilians danced to their rhythms. We found that at the popular dance halls generally they danced the Samba very much slower than we dance in this part of the world. Maybe the very hot climate has something to do with it or maybe they prefer it that way! We noticed that the Samba was a moving dance and at all the "dancings" we attended dancers progressed round the room as in English style. The only difference was that at the dance halls the music goes on and on, the dancers never stopping, especially where the coloured folk dance.

Like the Cubans the Brazilians are a very rhythmic nation. The first thing we saw upon our arrival in Rio was a street band, with instruments composed of tin cans, dustbin lids, and old saucepans, and they were certainly getting some pretty good rhythm from them.

On fête days—we were there for New Year's Eve—hundreds of bands play in the streets and the coloured Brazilians, dressed in very gay clothes, dance for many hours—and sometimes days—to the Marcha rhythm; sometimes this rhythm is mistaken for the Samba here.

The Brazilians dance solo or with arms around one another's waists, simply drunk with rhythm!

On our return to England we selected the most suitable figures we had learned there and combined them with other Samba figures popular in America. These figures form the basis of the syllabuses used by all Dancing Societies today.

SAMBA

The Samba is a moving dance and the dancers should travel round the room as they do in Waltz or Foxtrot.

Tempo. 48–54 bars per minute.

Musical Timing. 2/4 or 4/4. Many of the following figures are counted in beats, 1, 2, 1, 2, etc., but some figures are better counted in Slows and Quicks.

In the following pages where the musical timing is in 2/4 time (2 beats to each bar of music) and the timing is described as "1 and 2," the bar of music is divided as follows—

Step	Count	Beat Value
1	1	$\frac{3}{4}$
2	a	$\frac{1}{4}$
3	2	1

If the music is in 4/4 time (4 beats to one bar) the bar is divided as follows—

1	1	$1\frac{1}{2}$
2	a	$\frac{1}{2}$
3	2	2

Slows and Quicks in 2/4 timing—

1	Slow	1
2	Quick	$\frac{1}{2}$
3	Quick	$\frac{1}{2}$

Slows and Quicks in 4/4 timing—

Step	Count	Beat Value
1	Slow	2
2	Quick	1
3	Quick	1

The Hold. The gentleman holds the lady in normal ballroom hold but there is no hip contact.

Dropping Action. The Samba is usually in 2/4 time. On those figures where this action is applied a dropping movement (a slight flexing of the knees) is used on each beat of the music and a normal straightening occurs between each beat.

Natural Basic Movement

Entries. Any figure in the syllabus except Samba Walk in PP and Side Samba Walk.

Step	Feet Positions	Amount of Turn	Timing

Gentleman (commence with feet together and knees slightly relaxed. Use dropping action)

1	RF forward	No turn or turning approximately $\frac{1}{4}$ turn to right between steps 1 and 4	1 or S
2	LF closes to RF with pressure on LF		2 or S
3	LF back		1 or S
4	RF closes to LF with pressure on RF		2 or S

Reverse Basic Movement

As Natural Basic Movement but commencing with LF with no turn or turning approximately a quarter to left between steps 1 and 4.

Footwork. Ball flat or heel flat on steps 1 and ball flat on steps 2, 3 and 4.

Lady

Natural and Reverse Basic Movement, normal opposite.

Exits. Any figure in the syllabus except Samba Walk in PP or Side Samba Walk.

Natural Alternative Basic Movement

Entries. Any figure in the syllabus except Samba Walk in PP and Side Samba Walk.

Step	Feet Positions	Amount of Turn	Timing
Gentleman (use dropping action)			
1	RF forward	No turn or	1 or S
2	LF closes to RF, part weight	approximately ¼ turn to right	a
3	Replace full weight on RF	between steps 1 and 6	2 or S
4	LF back	—	1 or S
5	RF closes to LF, part weight	—	a
6	Replace full weight on LF	—	2 or S

Reverse Alternative Basic Movement

As Natural Alternative Basic Movement, but commencing with LF and turning approximately a quarter turn to left between steps 1 and 6.

Footwork. Ball flat or heel flat on step 1, and ball flat on steps 2 to 6.

Lady
Natural and Reverse Alternative Basic Movement, normal opposite.

Exits. Any figure in the syllabus, except Samba Walk in PP and Side Samba Walk.

Outside Basic Movement

Entry. Natural Basic Movement, Travelling Bota Fogo.

Step	Feet Positions	Amount of Turn	Timing
Gentleman (use dropping action)			
1	RF forward	None	1 or S
2	LF closes to RF with pressure on LF	Approximately ¼ turn to left	2 or S

Step	Feet Positions	Amount of Turn	Timing
3	LF back, partner outside	None	1 or S
4	RF closes to LF with pressure on RF	None	2 or S
5	RF forward outside partner	None	1 or S
6	LF closes to RF with pressure on LF	Approximately ¼ turn to right	2 or S
7	LF back	None	1 or S
8	RF closes to LF with pressure on LF	None	2 or S

Footwork. Ball flat or heel flat on steps 1 and 5, and ball flat on steps 2, 3, 4, 6, 7, 8.

Lady

Normal opposite except that on step 2 she turns approximately a quarter to left and on step 6 approximately a quarter to right.

Exit. Natural Basic Movement.

Progressive Basic Movement

Entries. Basic Movement or Progressive Basic Movement.

Step	Feet Positions	Amount of Turn	Timing

Gentleman (slight dropping action may be used. Commence facing diagonally to wall)

1	RF forward	None	1 or S
2	LF closes to RF with pressure on LF	None	2 or S
3	LF to side	None	1 or S
4	RF closes to LF with pressure on RF	None	2 or S

Footwork. Ball flat on steps 2 to 4, heel flat on step 1.

SAMBA—PROGRESSIVE BASIC MOVEMENT (FORWARD)
Steps 1 and 2
Steps 3 and 4

Lady
Normal opposite commenced backing diagonally to wall.

Exits. Basic Movement or Corta Jaca, or Change Step.

Change Step

Entry. Progressive Basic Movement, commenced facing diagonally to wall.

Step	Feet Positions	Amount of Turn	Timing
Gentleman			
1	RF forward (pivoting action)	Approximately ¼ turn to right	1 or S
2	LF back and slightly to side	None	2 or S

Footwork. Heel flat on step 1, ball flat on step 2.

Lady
Normal opposite.
Footwork. Ball flat on step 1, heel flat on step 2.

Exit. Backward Progressive Basic Movement.

Backward Progressive Basic Movement

Entry. Change step.

Step	Feet Positions	Amount of Turn	Timing

Gentleman (slight dropping action may be used. Commence backing diagonally to centre)

1	RF back	None	1 or S
2	LF closes to RF with pressure on LF	None	2 or S
3	LF to side	None	1 or S
4	RF closes to LF with pressure on RF	None	2 or S

Footwork. Ball flat on each step.

Lady
Normal opposite commenced facing diagonally to centre.

Footwork. Heel flat on step 1, ball flat on steps 2 to 4.

Exit. Second half Reverse Basic Movement, Bow and Reverse Turn.

Samba Whisk to Right

Entries. Natural Basic Movements. The figure is usually commenced with the gentleman facing and the lady backing the wall and when the gentleman commences with his RF the lady commences with her LF and vice versa.

Step	Feet Positions	Amount of Turn	Timing
	Gentleman and Lady (use dropping action)		
1	RF to side	None	1 or S
2	LF placed behind RF, L toe to R heel	None	a
3	Replace weight on RF	None	2 or S

Footwork. Ball flat on steps 1 and 3 and toe on step 2.

Samba Whisk to Left

Entries. Reverse Basic Movement and Samba Walk in PP. Samba Whisk to R.

Step	Feet Positions	Amount of Turn	Timing
	Gentleman and Lady (use dropping action)		
1	LF to side	None	1 or S
2	RF placed behind LF, R toe to L heel	None	a
3	Replace weight on LF	None	2 or S

Footwork. Ball flat on steps 1 and 3 and toe on step 2.
Exits. Basic Movement, Samba Walk in PP.

Samba Walk in Promenade Position

This movement is danced progressing along L.O.D. with the gentleman facing L.O.D. No dropping action is used.
Entries. Right Whisk, Promenade Bota Fogo.

Step	Feet Positions	Amount of Turn	Timing
Gentleman			
1	LF forward in PP slightly relaxing knee and leaving RF in place	None	1 or S
2	RF back, small step, part weight, straightening knee	None	a
3	Pull LF back 2 or 3 inches, replacing full weight on LF, knee straight	None	2 or S

A slight hip action is used in this figure as follows: step 1 hips forward, step 2 hips slightly back, step 3 hips normal position.

Repeat commencing with RF in PP. Samba Walks in PP can be repeated *ad lib*.

Footwork. Ball flat on step 1, ball on step 2, whole foot on step 3.

Note. The hold is rather high, gentleman's left hand is about level with his left ear, and the shoulders are kept steady throughout.

Lady

Same steps but with opposite feet. Body facing diagonally to centre on each step.

Exits. Left Whisk, Promenade Bota Fogo.

Corta Jaca

Entries. Basic Movement, Progressive Basic Movement, Whisk to left, Rocks.

Step	Feet Positions	Amount of Turn	Timing

Gentleman (this movement is usually danced facing wall. There is no dropping action)

THE SAMBA

SAMBA—CORTA JACA

Steps 1–3
Steps 4 and 5

1	RF forward	None	S
2	LF forward and slightly to side, straightening left knee and slightly bending right knee	None	Q
3	RF slides leftwards, right knee still relaxed	None	Q

Steps	Feet Positions	Amount of Turn	Timing
4	LF back and slightly to side, bending left knee	None	Q
5	RF slides leftwards, right knee still relaxed	None	Q

Repeat steps 2, 3, 4, 5, then repeat steps 2 and 3.

Footwork. Heel flat on step 1, heel on step 2, whole foot on steps 3 and 5, ball on step 4.

Lady (this movement is usually danced backing wall)

1	LF back	None	S
2	RF back and slightly to side, bending right knee and slightly relaxing left knee	None	Q
3	LF slides rightwards, left knee still relaxed	None	Q
4	RF forward and slightly to side straightening right knee, left knee still relaxed	None	Q
5	LF slides rightwards left knee still relaxed	None	Q

Repeat steps 2, 3, 4, 5, then steps 2 and 3.

Footwork. Ball flat on step 1, ball on step 2, whole foot on steps 3 and 5, heel on step 4.

Exits. Natural Basic Movement (second half) Natural Roll (second half).

Note. Although the swinging movement comes partly from the knee the upper part of the leg must be allowed to move freely and naturally.

THE SAMBA

Closed Rocks

Entries. Basic Movement, Natural Roll.

Step	Feet Positions	Amount of Turn	Timing

Gentleman (this movement is danced facing L.O.D. There is no dropping action)

1	RF forward	None	S
2	LF forward	None	Q
3	Replace weight on RF	None	Q

Footwork. Heel flat or ball flat on step 1, ball flat on steps 2 and 3.

Lady (commences backing L.O.D.)

1	LF back	None	S
2	RF back, toe close to heel, foot turned out, turning hips to right, shoulders square to partner		Q
3	Replace weight on LF		Q

Repeat above steps on opposite feet, commencing LF forward as gentleman, RF back as lady, thus completing two rocks.

SAMBA—CLOSED ROCKS, Steps 1–3

Footwork. Ball flat on steps 1 and 3, ball on step 2.

Step 3 (lady and gentleman) can also be danced by drawing the foot 2 or 3 inches towards the other foot.

Exits. Basic Movement, Corta Jaca, Open Rocks, Natural Roll, Reverse Turn.

Promenade Bota Fogo

Entries. Reverse Basic Movement, Samba Walk in PP.

Step	Feet Positions	Amount of Turn	Timing

Gentleman (usually commences facing wall). Use dropping action

1	LF forward	None	1 or S
2	RF to side with part weight	$\frac{1}{8}$ turn to left between steps 2 and 3	a
3	Replace full weight on LF in PP	—	2 or S
4	RF forward and across in PP	None	1 or S
5	LF to side with part weight	Commence to turn to right	a
6	Replace full weight on RF in CPP	Continue to turn to right making $\frac{1}{4}$ turn between steps 5 and 6	2 or S
7	LF forward and across in CPP	None	1 or S

Repeat steps 2 and 3, but turning $\frac{1}{4}$ to left thus completing three Bota Fogos.

Footwork. Ball flat or heel flat on steps 1, 4, 7, ball flat on steps 3 and 6, ball on steps 2 and 5.

Lady (usually commences backing wall). Use dropping action

1	RF back	None	1 or S
2	LF to side part weight	$\frac{1}{8}$ turn to right between steps 2 and 3	a
3	Replace full weight on RF		2 or S

THE SAMBA

4	LF forward and across in PP	None	1 or S
5	RF to side with part weight	Commence to turn to left	a
6	Replace full weight on LF	Continue to turn to left making $\frac{1}{4}$ turn between steps 5 and 6	2 or S
7	RF forward and across in CPP	None	1 or S

Repeat steps 2 and 3, but turning $\frac{1}{4}$ to right, thus completing three Bota Fogos.

Footwork. Ball flat on steps 1, 3, 6, ball on steps 2 and 5, ball flat or heel flat on steps 4 and 7.

Exits. Natural Basic, Samba Walk in PP.

Bow

Entries. Basic Movement, Backward Walk, Plait, Reverse Turn, Revirado.

Step	Feet Positions	Amount of Turn	Timing
Gentleman			
1	LF forward, leaning slightly forward from waist	Commence to turn to left	S
2	RF to side	Continue to turn to make approximately $\frac{1}{8}$ turn to left between steps 1 and 3	Q
3	LF closes to RF		Q
4	RF back, leaning slightly back	Continue to turn to left	S
5	LF to side	Continue to turn to make approximately $\frac{1}{8}$ turn to left between steps 4 and 6	Q
6	RF closes to LF		Q

Lady

Normal opposite, dancing steps 4, 5, 6, as gentleman dances steps 1, 2, 3, and vice versa.

Footwork. Ball flat or heel flat on step 1, ball flat on steps 2 to 6.

Note. The couple dance in rather close position but without actual hip contact. The leaning must be slight from the waist upwards, there is no side leaning or sway.

Exits. Basic Movement, Travelling Bota Fogo, Reverse Turn, or Travelling Bota Fogo backwards, Backward Walk, and Plait after dancing steps 1, 2, 3.

Reverse Turn

Entries. Basic Movement, Backward Walk, Plait, Bow.

Step	*Feet Positions*	*Amount of Turn*	*Timing*
Gentleman			
1	LF forward	Commence to turn to left	S or 1
2	RF to side	Continue to turn to left	Q or a
3	LF crosses over RF	Continue to turn to left leaning to L	Q or 2
4	RF back	Continue to turn to left	S or 1
5	LF to side small step	Continue to turn to left leaning to R, making up to a full turn between steps 1 and 6	Q or a
6	RF closes to LF		Q or 2

Lady

Normal opposite, dancing steps 4, 5, 6, as gentleman dances steps 1, 2, 3, and vice versa.

Footwork. Heel flat or ball flat on step 1, ball flat on steps 2, 3, 4, 5, 6.

Notes. A very slight dropping action can be used on steps 3 and 6. I favour for quicker rhythm the timing of 1 a 2.

Exits. Basic Movement, Travelling Bota Fogo, or Travelling Bota Fogo Backward, Backward Walk and Plait after dancing steps 1, 2, 3, Bow.

Side Samba Walk

This movement is usually danced facing L.O.D.
Entry. Samba Walk in PP.

Step	Feet Positions	Amount of Turn	Timing

Gentleman (after left foot Samba Walk in PP)

1	RF forward	None	1
2	LF to side	None	a
3	Draw RF 2 or 3 inches towards LF	None	2

Lady
Normal opposite in PP.

Footwork. Ball flat on step 1, ball on step 2, whole foot with pressure on ball of foot on step 3.

Exits. Samba Walk in PP, Stationary Samba Walk and Volta.

Note. The Side Samba Walk is used as an entry for many popular variations.

Stationary Samba Walk

This movement is usually danced facing wall.
Entry. Side Samba Walk, turning $\frac{1}{4}$ to R on step 3.

Step	Feet Positions	Amount of Turn	Timing

Gentleman (following Side Samba Walk turning to face partner. There is no dropping action)

1	LF closes to RF	None	1
2	RF back	None	a
3	Draw LF 2 or 3 inches towards RF	None	2
4	RF closes slightly in advance of LF	None	1
5	LF back	None	a
6	Draw RF 2 or 3 inches towards LF	None	2

Repeat steps 4, 5, 6, on alternate feet *ad lib.*, the three steps form the stationary Samba Walk.

Lady

Same steps but with opposite feet. This movement is usually danced backing wall.

Footwork. Ball flat on steps 1 and 4, ball on steps 2 and 5, whole foot on steps 3 and 6.

Exits. Whisk, Bota Fogo, Samba Walk in line.

Samba Walk in Line

Entries. Natural or Reverse Basic Movements.

Step   Feet Positions   Amount of Turn   Timing

Gentleman (This movement is danced in rather close position and usually facing L.O.D.)

1	RF forward slightly relaxing knee, leaving LF in place	None	1
2	LF back small step with part weight and straightening knees	None	a
3	Pull RF back 2 or 3 inches, replacing full weight on RF, knees straight	None	2

This movement may be repeated commencing with LF.

Footwork. Ball flat on step 1, ball on step 2, whole foot on step 3.

Lady. Normal opposite (usually backing L.O.D.).

This movement may be repeated commencing with RF.

Footwork. Ball flat on step 1, ball on step 2, whole foot on step 3.

Note. A slight hip action is used in this figure as follows: Forward on step 1, slightly back on step 2, normal position on step 3. The hip action for the lady is the normal opposite of the gentleman.

Exits. Basic Movements, Bow, Reverse Turn, Bota Fogo.

The Backward Rocks

This movement is danced in rather close position and moves backwards along L.O.D.

Entries. First half of Reverse Basic Movement, Bow, Reverse Turn, finishing back L.O.D.

Step	Feet Positions	Amount of Turn	Timing
Gentleman			
1	RF back	Left shoulder moves slightly back giving the feeling of a slight turn to left	S
2	Rock forward LF leaving RF in place	$\frac{1}{8}$ turn to left	Q
3	Replace weight on RF	$\frac{1}{8}$ turn to right	Q

This movement can be repeated commencing with the LF, and making one-eighth of a turn to right.

Lady
Normal opposite (facing L.O.D.).

Footwork. Ball flat on steps 1 and 3, ball on step 2.

Exits. Second half Basic Movements, Bow, and Plait.

Note. There is a very slight bounce on steps 2 and 3.

Travelling Bota Fogo Forward

This movement is usually danced progressing along L.O.D. with gentleman facing L.O.D. Dropping action is used, if timing is 1 and 2.

Entries. Reverse Basic Movement, Bow, Reverse Turn.

Step	Feet Positions	Amount of Turn	Timing
Gentleman			
1	LF forward	None	1 or S
2	RF to side with part weight	$\frac{1}{8}$ turn to left between steps 2 and 3	a

Step	Feet Positions	Amount of Turn	Timing
3	Replace full weight on LF		2 or S
4	RF forward, outside partner on right side	None	1 or S
5	LF to side, part weight	¼ turn to right between steps	a
6	Replace full weight on RF	5 and 6	2 or S

Steps 7, 8, 9, repeat steps 1, 2, 3, stepping forward outside partner on L side and making a quarter turn to left between steps 2 and 3, thus completing three Bota Fogos, 1 and 2 or S and S.

Footwork. Ball flat or heel flat on steps 1 and 4, ball on steps 2 and 5, ball flat on steps 3 and 6.

Lady (commences backing L.O.D.)

1	RF back	None	1 or S
2	LF to side with part weight	⅛ turn to left between steps	a
3	Replace full weight on RF	2 and 3	2 or S
4	LF back	None	1 or S
5	RF to side with part weight	¼ turn to right between steps	a
6	Replace full weight on LF	5 and 6	2 or S

Steps 7, 8, 9, normal opposite of gentleman's steps.

Footwork. Ball flat on steps 1, 3, 4, 6, and ball on steps 2 and 5.

Note. The timing SQQ instead of 1 a 2 can be used, especially to a slow tempo; there would then only be a slight dropping action and less turn on each Bota Fogo.

Exit. Outside Basic, Outside Change Step.

Travelling Bota Fogo Backward

Gentleman (after Outside Change Step, from Bota Fogo Forward, as described on page 58. Dropping action is used)

Steps 7, 8, 9 and 4, 5, 6, of lady's Travelling Bota Fogo Forward.

Samba—Travelling Bota Fogo
Steps 1 and 2
Steps 3 and 4

Lady

Steps number 7, 8, 9 and 4, 5, 6, gentleman's Travelling Bota Fogo Forward.

Exits. Cruzados, Outside Basic.

When Travelling Bota Fogo Backward follows the Travelling Bota Fogo Forward the Outside Change Step is used.

Note. If the timing of SQQ is used then there would only be a slight dropping action.

Outside Change Step

Step	Feet Positions	Amount of Turn	Timing
Gentleman (commencing facing L.O.D.)			
1	RF forward outside partner (pivoting action)	Approximately $\frac{3}{8}$ turn to right	1 or S
2	LF back and slightly to side	None	2 or S

Footwork. Heel flat on step 1, ball flat on step 2.

Lady

Normal opposite.

Open Rocks

This movement usually commences facing L.O.D.

Entries. Basic Movements, Rocks.

Step	Feet Positions	Amount of Turn	Timing
Gentleman			
1	RF forward	None	S
2	LF forward	None	Q
3	Replace weight on RF	None	Q

Repeat above three steps commencing with LF.

Footwork. Heel flat on step 1, ball flat on steps 2 and 3.

Note. Whilst the steps are the same for gentleman as the ordinary rocks the hold is different. The lady is swinging

THE SAMBA

alternately to the crook of gentleman's right arm, then to the crook of his left arm releasing hold from other hand.

Lady (this movement is danced backing L.O.D.)

1	LF back	Commence to turn to right	S
2	RF back and slightly to side	Continue to turn to right making approximately ½ turn between steps 1 and 2 and finish facing same way as gentleman	Q
3	LF forward small step	Commence to turn to left	Q
4	RF side and slightly back	Continue turning to left making approximately ½ turn between steps 3 and 4 and finish approximately facing partner	S
5	LF back and slightly to side	Continue turning to left making approximately ½ turn and finish facing same way as gentleman	Q
6	RF forward small step	Commence to turn to right	Q

Footwork. Ball flat on steps 1 to 6.

Note. Alternatively on steps 3 and 6 lady can replace the weight. On steps 2 and 3 the lady's right arm must be held naturally with arm slightly bent at the elbow, on steps 5 and 6 the lady's left arm must be held in the same way.

The Cruzado (Quadrado Cruzado)

This movement is usually commenced backing diagonally to centre.

Entry. Backward Bota Fogo finishing back on RF.

Step	Feet Positions	Amount of Turn	Timing
Gentleman			
1	LF back (partner outside on right side)	None	S
2	Cross RF loosely behind LF	Commence to turn to left	Q
3	LF to side and slightly forward	Continue to turn to left making ¼ turn between steps 2 and 3	Q
4	RF forward (outside partner on her right side)	None	S
5	LF crosses loosely in front of RF	Commence to turn to left	Q
6	RF to side and slightly back	Continue to turn to left making ¼ turn between steps 5 and 6	Q

Footwork. Ball flat on steps 1 and 4, ball on steps 2, 3, 5, 6.

Lady

Normal opposite (usually commenced facing diagonally to centre) dancing the 4th, 5th and 6th steps as her partner dances the 1st, 2nd and 3rd steps and vice versa.

Note. The Cruzado is danced with a slight dropping movement on each step similar to the Polka rhythm in the English Quickstep.

Exit. Repeat steps 1 to 6 and then 1 to 3 and finish with the forward half of the Natural Basic Movement, moving into line with partner. This could be followed with the Bow, Reverse Turn or Revirado.

THE SAMBA

Plait

The Brazilian name is *o trancadinho*, pronounced transadjinio. This movement is danced backing L.O.D. and the hold is slightly apart.

Entry. Backward walk, or after first 3 steps of Bow and Reverse Turn.

Step   *Feet Positions*   *Amount of Turn*   *Timing*

Gentleman

1	RF back	None	S
2	LF back	None	S
3	RF back	None	Q
4	LF back	None	Q
5	RF back	None	S

These five steps can be repeated commencing with LF.

Footwork. Ball flat on steps 1 to 5.

Lady (This movement is danced facing L.O.D.)

1	LF forward with toe turned out, swivelling on RF to left	$\frac{1}{8}$ turn to left	S
2	RF forward with toe turned out, swivelling on LF to right	$\frac{1}{4}$ turn to right	S
3	LF forward with toe turned out, swivelling on RF to left	$\frac{1}{4}$ turn to left	Q
4	RF forward with toe turned out, swivelling on LF to right	$\frac{1}{4}$ turn to right	Q
5	LF forward with toe turned out, swivelling on RF to left	$\frac{1}{4}$ turn to left	S

The five steps can be repeated commencing with RF.

Footwork. Ball of foot on steps 1 to 5.

Exits. Second half Basic Movements, Bow, Reverse Turn.

Note. The gentleman could use a slight swivelling action if desired and this would be as follows—
  Step 1. Slight swivel to left
  Step 2. Slight swivel to right
  Step 3. Slight swivel to left
  Step 4. Slight swivel to right
  Step 5. Slight swivel to left.

The Revirado

This movement is usually commenced facing L.O.D.

Entries. Forward half Natural Basic, Backward half Reverse Basic, Bow, Reverse Turn.

Step	Feet Positions	Amount of Turn	Timing
Gentleman			
1	LF forward outside partner (right hip to right hip)	None	S
2	RF closes to LF	None	Q
3	Transfer weight to LF	None	Q
4	RF forward outside partner	None	S
5	LF closes to RF	None	Q
6	Transfer weight to RF	None	Q
7, 8, 9	Repeat steps 1, 2, 3, L, R, L	None	S, Q, Q
10	RF forward finishing on partner's left side, that is left hip to left hip	½ turn to right	S
11	LF closes to RF	None	Q
12	Transfer weight to RF	None	Q

THE SAMBA

13	LF back partner outside on left side, left hip to left hip	None	S
14	RF closes to LF	None	Q
15	Transfer weight to LF	None	Q
16	RF back	None	S
17	LF closes to RF	None	Q
18	Transfer weight to RF	None	Q
19, 20, 21	Repeat steps 13, 14, 15, L, R, L	None	S, Q, Q
22	RF back finishing on partner's right side, that is right hip to right hip	½ turn to left	S
23	LF closes to RF	None	Q
24	Transfer weight to RF	None	Q

Footwork. Ball flat on each step, or heel flat can be used on steps 1, 4, 7, 10.

Lady

Normal opposite. On steps 10, 11, 12 when the gentleman makes half a turn to right stepping forward on his RF and changes the lady's position from his right to his left side, she dances as follows—

10	LF back	½ turn to right	S
11	RF closes to LF	None	Q
12	Transfer weight to LF	None	Q

Similarly when the gentleman changes the lady's position from his left to his right side she dances as follows—

22	LF forward	½ turn to left	S
23	RF closes to LF	None	Q
24	Transfer weight to LF	None	Q

Footwork. Ball flat on each step, or heel flat can be used on steps 13, 16, 19, 22.

Exits. Reverse Basic Movement, Bow, Reverse Turn.

Amalgamation

Gentleman

Commence facing diagonally to wall with right foot.

Forward and back Basic Movement, four times. Finish facing diagonally to wall.

Progressive Basic Movement, twice, finish facing diagonally to wall.

Corta Jaca, commencing forward RF, facing wall, finish with back basic and still facing wall.

Right Whisk, facing wall.

Left Whisk, facing wall.

Right Whisk, finish facing L.O.D.

Samba Walk in PP, four times and turning to face wall on the fourth.

Left Whisk, facing wall.

Natural Basic Movement, three times, finish facing L.O.D.

Closed Rocks, four times, finish facing L.O.D.

Forward Basic Movement, no turn, facing L.O.D.

Travelling Bota Fogo, three times, finish facing diagonally to centre and with lady now on gentleman's right side.

Outside Basic, once, finish facing diagonally to wall.

Repeat from beginning.

Note. This amalgamation would fit a fairly long room. For a smaller room the forward and back basic which I have suggested could be danced three times, if danced twice, would enable the dancers to use a new line of dance.

Lady

Normal opposite except when the gentleman dances the whisk to the right and turns into PP. The lady when dancing the whisk to the left would also turn into PP. The lady and gentleman would then be facing in the same direction.

SAMBA VARIATIONS

The Natural Roll

There is no dropping action in this variation.

Entries. Basic Movement, Corta Jaca, Rocks.

THE SAMBA

Step	Feet Positions	Amount of Turn	Timing
Gentleman			
1	RF forward, leaning slightly back from waist	Commence to turn to right	S
2	LF to side, leaning slightly to right	Continue to turn to right	Q
3	RF closes to LF preparing to lean forward	Slight turn to right	Q
4	LF back, leaning slightly forward	Turning to right	S
5	RF to side, leaning slightly to left	Continue to turn to right	Q
6	LF closes to RF preparing to lean back	Turning to right	Q

Footwork. Heel flat on step 1, and ball flat on steps 2, 3, 4, 5, 6.

The amount of turn varies from half to a whole turn over the six steps.

Lady

Normal opposite, dancing steps 4, 5, 6, while gentleman dances 1, 2, 3, and vice versa.

Exits. Basic Movement, Corta Jaca, Rocks, Maxixe.

Note. This figure may also be danced turning to the left and would be commenced LF for gentleman and back RF for lady. The Rolls either to right or left are hardly ever seen nowadays in Brazilian ballrooms. The modern version is the Bow, which has been described earlier.

The Volta (Turn)

This movement is danced in fairly close hold, and can be commenced also with the LF.

Entries. Forward half of Reverse Basic, Whisk, Samba Walk in PP, Side Samba Walk.

66 LATIN AND AMERICAN DANCES

Step	*Feet Positions*	*Amount of Turn*	*Timing*
Gentleman			
1	Place R heel to toe of LF (R toe turned out)	Commence to turn slightly to left	1 or S
2	Move LF back about 3 inches	Continue to turn slightly to left	a
3	Draw R heel to L toe	Continue to turn slightly to left	2 or S
4	Move LF back about 3 inches	Continue to turn slightly to left	a
5	Draw R heel to L toe	Continue to turn slightly to left	3 or S
6	Move LF back about 3 inches	Continue to turn slightly to left	a
7	Draw R heel to L toe	Continue to turn slightly to left	4 or S

Note. The seven movements R, L, R, L, R, L, R (1 and 2 and 3 and 4) complete the first half of the Volta and the following points must be carefully observed—

On count 1 the movement is commenced by moving the RF forward with no weight, a fraction before placing the R heel to L toe. Both knees must be kept bent to ensure proper control of the feet. The body is bent to the right, that is towards the foot that is being drawn to the other on each count (in this case the RF). The weight is on the right on each count, that is on counts 1, 2, 3, 4. The weight is on the LF on each count of a. The RF and LF are almost at right-angles. The second half of the Volta is as follows—

8	Swivel on ball of RF at the same time placing the L heel to the R toe (L toe turned out)	$\frac{1}{8}$ turn to left	1 or S
9	Move RF to side and slightly back	Continue to turn slightly to left	a
10	Draw L heel to R toe	Continue to turn slightly to left	2 or S

THE SAMBA

11	Move RF to side and slightly back	Continue to turn slightly to left	a
12	Draw L heel to R toe	Continue to turn slightly to left	3 or S
13	Move RF to side and slightly back	Continue to turn slightly to left	a
14	Draw L heel to R toe	Continue to turn slightly to left	4 or S

Note. The last seven movements L, R, L, R, L, R, L (1 and 2 and 3 and 4) complete the second half of the Volta and the following points must be observed. Both knees must be bent. The body is bent to the left from the waist, that is towards the LF. The weight is on the left on each count of 1, 2, 3, 4, and on the right on each count of a. The first and second half of the Volta can be repeated.

Footwork. Flat on steps 1, 3, 5, 7, 8, 10, 12, 14, ball of foot on steps 2, 4, 6, 9, 11, 13.

Lady

The lady's first half of the Volta is the same as the gentleman's second half, and her second half the same as the gentleman's first half.

Exit. Backward Half Reverse Basic, Whisk.

Bota Fogo Cum Batu Variation (or Change of Feet)

Step *Feet Positions* *Amount of Turn* *Timing*

Gentleman (commence with Bota Fogo L, R, L, count 1 and 2, and usually commences facing wall)

1	RF forward and across in PP	⅛ turn to left	1
2	LF moves towards RF about 2 or 3 inches	None	a
3	RF forward short step	None	2
4	LF moves towards RF 2 or 3 inches	None	a

Footwork. Heel or ball flat on steps 1 and 3, ball of foot on steps 2 and 4.

Continue with Bota Fogo commencing with RF and turning to right. The gentleman is now on the same foot as the lady and moving in opposition. Instead of this movement the gentleman can point RF forward (no weight) count 1, RF back (no weight) count 2, or short step forward RF followed by a short step forward LF count 1, 2.

Lady
The lady dances Bota Fogo throughout.

After the gentleman has danced the Cum Batu the lady and gentleman can continue dancing the Bota Fogo, both commencing with the left foot. The gentleman can then repeat the Cum Batu whilst the lady dances a Bota Fogo R, L, R, and this brings them back on opposite feet.

Exit. Bota Fogo, gentleman R, L, R, lady L, R, L.

The Point Variation

This figure is usually commenced facing L.O.D. It is useful for social dancing or for Silver and Gold medallist standard.

Entry. Travelling Bota Fogo L, R, L, 1 and 2.

Step	Feet Positions	Amount of Turn	Timing
Gentleman			
1	RF forward outside partner	None	1
2	Point LF forward without weight	None	2
3	LF closes to RF	None	1
4	RF back small step	None	a
5	Draw LF back 2 or 3 inches towards RF	None	2

These five steps can be repeated two or three times.

To finish, dance the outside Basic Movement R, L, swivelling to face partner as LF closes to RF.

Footwork. Heel flat on step 1, toe on step 2, ball flat on step 3, ball of foot on step 4, whole foot on step 5.

Lady
Normal opposite.

Maxixe Variation

This movement is only suitable for competitions or demonstrations.

Gentleman

Entry. Natural Roll, 1, 2, 3, 4, 5, 6, S, Q, Q, S, Q, Q. The lady's right hand is in his right hand at waist level and behind the lady's back, her left hand in his left hand are raised above the heads. Forward RF, 7, S, and leading with his right hand the gentleman turns the lady half a turn to the right to finish in a position on his right side, his right hand still holding her right hand round her waist and his left hand holding her left hand about level with his ear (they are now both facing the same direction).

SAMBA—MAXIXE VARIATION
Entry (Brazilian Hold)

70　　　LATIN AND AMERICAN DANCES

Step	Feet Positions	Amount of Turn	Timing
1	LF to side	Commence to turn to right	Q
2	RF closes to LF	None	Q
3	LF to side lifting RF off the floor pointing toe backwards keeping knees together and bending to the right	Still turning slightly to right	S
4	RF to side, body straightening	Still turning slightly to right	Q

SAMBA—MAXIXE VARIATION
Steps 1–3
Steps 4–6

THE SAMBA

5	LF closes to RF	None	Q
6	RF to side bending right knee in a sitting position with upper part of body upright, straightening left leg and pointing toe forwards.	Still turning slightly to right	S

Repeat steps 1 to 6 two or three times.

Footwork. Ball flat on each step.

Lady

Entry. Natural Roll, on the 7th step (LF back) turn half turn to right transferring weight to RF, count Q, Q, to finish facing the same direction as the gentleman. To continue, dance steps 1 to 6 the same as gentleman and repeat two or three times.

Flying Angel Variation

This movement is only suitable for competitions or demonstrations.

Entry. Natural Basic Movement or Closed Rocks.

Step	Feet Positions	Amount of Turn	Timing
Gentleman			
1	RF forward	None	S
2	LF to side and slightly forward and swinging left shoulder and hip slightly forward	None	Q
3	Draw RF almost to LF squaring shoulders and hips	None	Q
4	LF back	None	S

72   LATIN AND AMERICAN DANCES

SAMBA—THE FLYING ANGEL
Above: Steps 1–3; *Below:* Steps 4 and 5

Step	Feet Positions	Amount of Turn	Timing
5	Lift partner with the help of right hand and leg, lean slightly back raising right leg with toe pointing downwards	None	S

Footwork. Heel flat on step 1, ball flat on steps 2, 3, 4, and flat on step 5.

Lady

1	LF back	None	S

2	RF side and slightly back swinging right shoulder and right hip slightly back	None	Q
3	Draw LF almost to RF straightening shoulders and hips	None	Q
4	RF forward and bending right knee	None	S
5	Spring lightly up from right leg	None	S

Footwork. Ball flat on each step.

Note. On step 5 the lady is helped by leaning her left thigh against her partner.

EXAMINATION QUESTIONS AND ANSWERS

Samba for Associates

Basic Movement

Q. On which counts is the dropping action used?

A. The dropping action is used on each beat of the music count 1, 2, 1, 2.

Q. Give a common fault.

A. Taking the step forward with a straight knee and only dropping on count 2.

Progressive Basic

Q. Give the alignment in which this step is usually danced.

A. Facing diagonally to wall.

Q. Is the dropping action used in this step?

A. Yes, but only slightly.

Corta Jaca

Q. Count the Corta Jaca in beats, 2/4 time.

A. Step forward RF count 1, then 2 and 1 and 2 and 1 and 2 and, step back LF count 1, close RF to LF count 2.

Q. How would it be counted in slows and quicks?

A. SQQQQQQQQQQSS.

Q. Give a common fault.

A. Dancing in the rhythm of $\frac{3}{4}$ and $\frac{1}{4}$ beats when dancing the heel and toe movements, instead of $\frac{1}{2}$ and $\frac{1}{2}$ beats.

The Samba Whisks

Q. Is there any turn in this figure?

A. Usually no, but if followed by the Samba Walk in PP, the turn is made on step 3.

Samba Walk in PP

Q. Describe the Samba Walk commencing with RF.

A. RF forward swinging the hips slightly forward count 1, LF back 2 or 3 inches count "and," draw RF towards LF bringing hips back to normal position count 2.

Closed Rocks

Q. Does the lady's head turn when the first step is taken?

A. No, there would be no reason for this because the shoulders are kept practically square with her partner throughout the figure.

Bota Fogo (Travelling)

Q. Should this step be counted 1 and 2 or SQQ?

THE SAMBA

A. SQQ when the music is slow or medium slow, but when fast or medium it is counted 1 and 2.

Q. If the music is slow is the dropping action employed?

A. No, the dropping action is more suitable to faster music.

Bow

Q. Should the steps be small?

A. Yes, because the character of this figure is shown in the strong lean forward on step 1 and back on step 4.

Members' and Fellows' Syllabus

Reverse Turn

Q. How much turn is made?

A. Up to a full turn. A full turn is usually made when dancing the slow Samba but less when the music is fast.

Q. Is the dropping action used in this figure?

A. A slight drop is made on steps 3 and 6.

Side Samba Walk

Q. What is the lead for this figure?

A. The gentleman leads the lady with his right hand to take a step with her RF to the side instead of back as in the Samba Walk in PP. This step is taken on the count of "and."

Backward Walk

Q. Is the figure the normal opposite of the Samba Walk Forward?

A. No, there are several differences as follows—

1. The timing of the Backward Walk is SQQ and the Samba Walk 1 and 2.

2. The hips swing forward and back slightly in the Samba Walk but when dancing the Backward Walk the hips do not swing, but a slight CBM is used on the count of slow.

3. When dancing the Samba Walk the poise is upright but in the Backward Walk the weight is slightly forward.

Open Rocks

Q. Are the gentleman's steps the same as in the Closed Rocks?

A. Yes, but the first step—Slow—is a little shorter.

Cruzado

Q. In what alignments can this be taken?

A. It can be commenced backing diagonally to centre and finished facing diagonally to wall, having danced five SQQs, and turned $1\frac{1}{4}$ turns to left, or commenced facing wall and finished facing L.O.D.

Plait

Q. Does the gentleman walk straight back or can he swivel his feet?

A. It is more correct for him to walk straight back, the step is named after the lady's movement.

Revirado

Q. On which foot does the gentleman make his half turn?

A. On the RF when moving forward, and the RF when moving back.

Q. Give an entry.

A. The Bow, by moving slightly on to the lady's right side as the RF closes to LF.

SECTION III

PASO DOBLE

The Paso Doble can be danced in two styles, firstly the authentic Spanish style as seen in Spain and secondly the style which was developed in France before the war. The latter has gained great popularity in England for demonstrations, competitions, professional examinations, and amateur medal tests.

Important features of this dance are precision of footwork and elegant deportment as seen in all Spanish dancing. The hold is a trifle higher than the normal ballroom hold and many of the figures have a light hip contact.

The first seven figures described could be danced in any country where the Paso Doble is played. It can be danced in a very small space. The last nine figures could be danced, but would have to be so condensed that they would possibly lose their character, for they portray the *Torero* fighting the bull and handling his cloak. The gentleman represents the *Torero* and the lady the cloak.

When dancing the second style, "arm movements" may be used but must never be exaggerated. For example in the déplacement, on step 4 when LF closes to RF the gentleman's left arm and lady's right arm can be lowered but not below waist level. This figure represents the *Torero* quickly stepping aside and lowering his cloak to avoid the bull.

PASO DOBLE

Tempo. 60 bars per minute.
Musical Timing. 2/4, 3/4 or 6/8.

2/4–1 step taken for each beat of music
3/4–1 step taken for each beat of music
6/8–1 step taken for 3 counts

    1, 2, 3, on first step
    4, 5, 6, on second step
    The steps are therefore taken on counts 1 and 4

In the descriptions of the steps it will be assumed that the timing is 2/4.

Basic Movement

This figure is danced with slight hip contact, moving backwards or forwards.

Entries. Sur Place, Chassés, Elevation, Huit, Sixteen.

Step	Feet Positions	Amount of Turn	Footwork	Timing
Gentleman				
1	RF forward small step	None or slight to right or left	Ball or ball flat	1 or S
2	LF forward small step	None or slight to right or left	Ball or ball flat	2 or S

Lady
Normal opposite moving backwards or forwards.
The above steps may be repeated *ad lib*.

Exits. Sur Place, Chassés, Elevation, Separation.

Sur Place

This figure is danced with slight hip contact, on the spot without progression.

Entries. All figures in the syllabus.

Step	Feet Positions	Amount of Turn	Footwork	Timing
Gentleman				
1	Step on RF keeping feet together	None or turn to right or left	Ball or ball flat	1 or S

PASO DOBLE

2	Step on LF keeping feet together	None or turn to right or left	Ball or ball flat	2 or S

The above steps can be repeated *ad lib*.

Lady
Normal opposite.
Exits. All figures in the syllabus.

Chassés to Right

This figure is usually danced backing wall and has slight hip contact.
Entries. Basic Movement, Sur Place, Elevation.

Step	Feet Positions	Amount of Turn	Footwork	Timing
Gentleman				
1	RF to side	None	Ball flat	1 or S
2	LF closes to RF	None	Ball flat	2 or S

Lady
Normal opposite.
The above steps may be repeated *ad lib*.
Exits. Basic Movement, Sur Place, Elevation.

Chassés to Left

This figure is danced facing wall and with slight hip contact.
Entries. Basic Movement, Sur Place, Elevation.

Step	Feet Positions	Amount of Turn	Footwork	Timing
Gentleman (precede with Sur Place on RF, count 1)				
2	LF to side	None	Ball flat	2 or S
3	RF closes to LF	None	Ball flat	1 or S

Lady
Normal opposite.
The above steps may be repeated *ad lib*.
Exits. Basic Movement, Sur Place, Elevation.

Elevation

This figure is danced moving rightwards along L.O.D., that is, backing wall.

Entries. Sur Place, Basic Movement.

Step	Feet Positions	Amount of Turn	Footwork	Timing
Gentleman				
1	RF to side, rising at end of step	None	Ball of foot	1 or S
2	LF closes to RF, up	None	Ball of foot	2 or S
3	RF to side lowering at end of step	None	Ball flat	1 or S
4	LF closes to RF, down	None	Ball flat	2 or S

Lady
Normal opposite.

Note. This figure can be danced several ways. One chassé up, one chassé down, timing 1, 2. Two chassés up, two chassés down, timing 1, 2, 1, 2, *or* up on beat 1 and down on beat 2. When moving leftwards along L.O.D. (gentleman facing wall) it would commence with an Appel on RF.

Exits. Sur Place, Basic Movement.

Déplacement

This figure can commence facing L.O.D., diagonally to centre or diagonally to wall and is danced with slight hip contact.

Entry. Sur Place.

Step	Feet Positions	Amount of Turn	Footwork	Timing
Gentleman				
1	RF forward	None	Heel flat	1 or S
2	LF forward	None	Heel flat	2 or S
3	RF to side	¼ turn to left	Ball flat	1 or S
4	LF closes to RF	None	Ball flat	2 or S

Lady
Normal opposite.

Exit. Sur Place.

Paso Doble—Déplacement
   Steps 1 and 2
   Steps 3 and 4

Note. The movement in the Déplacement is that of ordinary walking and a slight CBM may be used on steps 1, 2 and 3. The turn is optional.

The Huit (The Eight)

This figure can be commenced facing diagonally to wall.
Entries. Sur Place, Elevation, Chassés to Left.

Step	Feet Positions	Amount of Turn	Footwork	Timing
Gentleman				
1	RF forward and across in PP	None	Heel flat	1 or S
2	LF closes to RF	⅛ turn to right	Ball flat	2 or S
3–8	Mark time with feet together	None	Ball flat on each step	1, 2, 1, 2, 1, 2, or S, S, S, S, S, S

The gentleman keeps a high hold throughout the Huit and leads mostly with his right hand which he keeps on the lady's back as in normal hold.

	Lady (Facing diagonally to centre)			
1	LF forward and across in PP	None	Heel flat	1 or S
2	RF to side	Approximately ⅛ turn to left	Ball of foot	2 or S
3	Replace weight on LF in place	Approximately ⅛ turn to left	Ball flat	1 or S
4	RF forward and across in CPP	None	Heel flat	2 or S
5	LF to side	Approximately ⅛ turn to right	Ball of foot	1 or S
6	Replace weight on RF in place	Approximately ⅛ turn to right	Ball flat	2 or S
7	LF forward in PP	None	Heel flat	1 or S
8	RF closes to LF	⅛ turn to left	Ball flat	2 or S

The lady uses a marching action with her supporting knee slightly relaxed. Her position is slightly lower than her partner which helps to give the "cape" effect. She resumes normal position on step 8.

Exit. Sur Place, Banderillas.

Appel

Entries. The Appel is used as an entry to certain figures.

Step	Feet Positions	Amount of Turn	Footwork	Timing
Gentleman				
1	Step on RF close to LF	None	Ball flat	1 or S

Lady
Normal opposite.
The couple are in closed position.

Exits. Elevation to Left, Sixteen, Separation, Sur Place, Elevation, Promenades, Ecart et Véronique, Twists.

The Separation

This figure can be commenced facing L.O.D.
Entry. Sur Place.

Step	Feet Positions	Amount of Turn	Footwork	Timing
Gentleman				
1	Step on RF close to LF (Appel)	None	Ball flat	1 or S
2	LF forward, rising at end of step	None	Heel ball	2 or S
3	RF closes to LF, releasing hold with right hand	None	Ball of foot	1 or S
4	Mark time with LF	None	Ball of foot	2 or S
5	Mark time with RF	None	Ball of foot	1 or S
6	Mark time with LF	None	Ball of foot	2 or S
7	Mark time with RF	None	Ball of foot	1 or S
8	Mark time with LF lowering at end of step	None	Ball flat	2 or S
Lady				
1	Step on LF close to RF (Appel)	None	Ball flat	1 or S

Paso Doble—Huit
Steps 1, 2
Steps 5, 6

Paso Doble—Huit
  Steps 3, 4
  Steps 7, 8

Step	Feet Positions	Amount of Turn	Footwork	Timing
2	RF back	None	Ball flat	2 or S
3	LF back, rising at end of step	None	Ball of foot	1 or S
4	RF closes to LF	None	Ball of foot	2 or S
5	LF forward	None	Ball of foot	1 or S
6	RF forward	None	Ball of foot	2 or S
7	LF forward	None	Ball of foot	1 or S
8	RF forward, lowering at end of step	None	Ball flat	2 or S

Note. The lady and gentleman must be careful not to move too far apart in this figure, the gentleman leads his partner to step back on step 3 by giving her a gentle push with his right hand and releasing hold with his right hand.

Exits. Sur Place, Basic Movement, or a popular finish to the Separation which is described below.

Advanced Ending to Separation (Following Ending)

Entry. Repeat the last eight steps as described in Separation but on steps 5, 6, 7, 8, lady moves to a position on her partner's right side, right hip to right hip.

Step	Feet Positions	Amount of Turn	Footwork	Timing
Gentleman				
1	RF forward on partner's right side	Commence to turn to right approximately ¼ turn	Heel flat	1 or S
2	LF forward outside partner	Continue to turn to right approximately ¼ turn	Ball flat	2 or S
3	RF back and slightly to side	Continue to turn to right approximately ⅛ turn	Ball flat	1 or S
4	LF back in Fallaway	None	Ball flat	2 or S
5	RF to side	Approximately ⅛ turn to right	Ball flat	1 or S
6	LF closes to RF	None	Ball flat	2 or S
7	RF to side	None	Ball flat	1 or S
8	LF closes to RF	None	Ball flat	2 or S

Paso Doble—Separation
Steps 1 and 2
Steps 3 and 4

Step	Feet Positions	Amount of Turn	Footwork	Timing
Lady				
1	LF forward on partner's right side	Commence to turn to right making approximately ¼ turn	Heel flat	1 or S
2	RF forward outside partner	Continue to turn to right making approximately ¼ turn	Ball flat	2 or S
3	LF back and slightly to side	Approximately ⅜ turn to right	Ball flat	1 or S
4	RF back in Fallaway	None	Ball flat	2 or S
5	LF to side	Approximately ⅛ turn to left	Ball flat	1 or S
6	RF closes to LF	None	Ball flat	2 or S
7	LF to side	None	Ball flat	1 or S
8	RF closes to LF	None	Ball flat	2 or S

The Sixteen

This figure is usually commenced facing wall with the lady and gentleman slightly apart.

Entries. Sur Place.

Step	Feet Positions	Amount of Turn	Footwork	Timing
Gentleman				
1	Step on RF close to LF (Appel)	None	Ball flat	1 or S
2	LF to side in PP	⅛ turn to left	Heel flat	2 or S
3	RF forward and across in PP	Commence to turn to right	Heel flat	1 or S
4	LF back and slightly to side	⅜ turn to right between steps 3 and 4	Ball flat	2 or S
5	RF back, commencing to lead partner outside on right side	None	Ball flat	1 or S
6	LF back	None	Ball flat	2 or S
7	RF closes to LF	¼ turn to right	Ball flat	1 or S
8	Step on LF	None	Ball flat	2 or S

PASO DOBLE—THE SIXTEEN
   Steps 1 and 2
   Steps 3 and 4

Step	Feet Positions	Amount of Turn	Footwork	Timing
9–16	Mark time on R, L, R, L, R, L, R, L	None	Ball flat on each step	1, 2, 1, 2, 1, 2, 1, 2 or S, S, S, S, S, S, S, S

Lady

Step	Feet Positions	Amount of Turn	Footwork	Timing
1	Step on LF close to RF (Appel)	None	Ball flat	1 or S
2	RF to side in PP	⅛ turn to right	Heel flat	2 or S
3	LF forward and across in PP	None	Heel flat	1 or S
4	RF forward	⅛ turn to right	Heel flat	2 or S
5	LF forward	None	Heel flat	1 or S
6	RF forward outside partner	None	Heel flat	2 or S
7	LF to side	¼ turn to right	Ball of foot	1 or S
8	Replace weight on RF in place	⅛ turn to right	Ball flat	2 or S
9	LF forward and across in PP	None	Heel flat	1 or S
10	RF to side	⅛ turn to left	Ball of foot	2 or S
11	Replace weight on LF in place	⅛ turn to left	Ball flat	1 or S
12	RF forward and across in CPP	None	Heel flat	2 or S
13	LF to side	⅛ turn to right	Ball of foot	1 or S
14	Replace weight on RF in place	⅛ turn to right	Ball flat	2 or S
15	LF forward in PP	None	Heel flat	1 or S
16	RF closes to LF	⅛ turn to left	Ball flat	2 or S

Exits. Sur Place, Basic Movement, Banderillas.

The Promenades

This movement is danced with the lady and gentleman slightly apart and is usually commenced facing wall.

Entry. Sur Place.

Step	Feet Positions	Amount of Turn	Footwork	Timing
Gentleman				
1	Step on RF (Appel)	None	Ball flat	1 or S
2	LF to side in PP	⅛ turn to left	Heel flat	2 or S

PASO DOBLE

3	RF forward and across in PP	Commence turning to right	Heel flat	1 or S
4	LF side and slightly back	⅜ turn to right between 3 and 4	Ball flat	2 or S
5	RF to side in CPP	⅛ turn to right	Heel flat	1 or S
6	LF forward and across in CPP	Turning right	Heel flat	2 or S
7	RF forward	⅛ turn to right between 6 and 7	Heel flat	1 or S
8	LF to side in PP	⅛ turn to left	Heel flat	2 or S

Lady

1	Step on LF (Appel)	None	Ball flat	1 or S
2	RF to side in PP	⅛ turn to right	Heel flat	2 or S
3	LF forward and across in PP	Turning right	Heel flat	1 or S
4	RF forward and slightly to side	⅛ turn to right between 3 and 4	Heel flat	2 or S
5	LF to side in CPP	⅛ turn to left	Heel flat	1 or S
6	RF forward and across in CPP	Turning right	Heel flat	2 or S
7	LF back and slightly to side	⅜ turn to right between 6 and 7	Ball flat	1 or S
8	RF to side in PP	⅛ turn to right	Heel flat	2 or S

Note. On the steps 4 and 7 the position of the lady's and gentleman's feet should be approximately toe to toe.

Exits. Sur Place, Advanced Ending as described below.

Advanced Ending to Promenades (Grand Circle)

Entry. After eight steps of the Promenades have been danced finishing LF to side in PP.

Step	Feet Positions	Amount of Turn	Footwork	Timing
Gentleman				
1	RF crosses over LF	None	Heel flat	1 or S

LATIN AND AMERICAN DANCES

Step	Feet Positions	Amount of Turn	Footwork	Timing
2–8	Swivel on balls of both feet finishing with RF behind LF	Approximately ½ turn to left	Ball of foot (feet flat)	2, 1, 2, 1, 2, 1, 2, or S, S, S, S, S, S, S
9	RF crosses smartly over LF	None	Heel flat	1 or S
10	Close LF to RF	None	Ball of foot	2 or S

Lady

1	LF forward and across in PP	None	Heel flat	1 or S
2–8	Continue with 7 short walking steps forward moving round partner as he swivels	Approximately ½ turn to left	Ball of foot	2, 1, 2, 1, 2, 1, 2, or S, S, S, S, S, S, S
9	LF forward	None	Heel flat	1 or S
10	RF closes to LF turning to face partner	Approximately ⅛ turn to left	Ball of foot	2 or S

Note. On steps 2 to 8 the gentleman holds his partner away from him to allow her to circle freely. The arms are held fairly high but are relaxed. This is one of the figures that interpret the *torero* and his cloak.

La Passe

Entry. Sur Place.

Step	Feet Positions	Amount of Turn	Footwork	Timing

Gentleman (after five steps of the Sixteen, commences this step backing L.O.D.)

				1, 2, 1, 2, 1, or S, S, S, S, S
6	LF back	Approximately ⅛ turn to right	Ball flat	2 or S
7	RF forward	Approximately ⅛ turn to right	Heel flat or Ball flat	1 or S
8	Hesitate			2 or S
9	Hesitate			1 or S

PASO DOBLE

10	LF forward	None	Heel flat or Ball flat	2 or S
11	Hesitate			1 or S
12	Hesitate			2 or S
13	RF forward	None	Heel or Ball flat	1 or S
14	Hesitate			2 or S
15	Hesitate			1 or S
16	LF closes to RF	None	Ball flat	2 or S

Lady (after five steps of the Sixteen, commence this step facing L.O.D.)

				1, 2, 1, 2, 1 or S, S, S, S, S
6	RF forward outside partner	Commence to turn to right	Heel flat	2 or S
7	LF to side	¼ turn to right between steps 6 and 7	Ball of foot	1 or S
8	RF to side	⅛ turn to right	Ball flat	2 or S
9	LF forward and across in PP	None	Heel flat	1 or S
10	RF forward	⅛ turn to left	Ball of foot	2 or S
11	LF to side	⅛ turn to left	Ball flat	1 or S
12	RF forward and across in CPP	None	Heel flat	2 or S
13	LF to side	⅛ turn to right	Ball of foot	1 or S
14	RF to side	⅛ turn to right	Ball flat	2 or S
15	LF forward in PP	None	Heel flat	1 or S
16	RF closes to LF	⅛ turn to left	Ball flat	2 or S

Exit. Sur Place, Banderillas.

Sur Place Elevation

Entries. Sur Place, Basic Movement.

Step	Feet Positions	Amount of Turn	Footwork	Timing
Gentleman				
1	Appel on RF	Slight body turn to left	Ball flat	1 or S
2	Step on LF	Commence to turn body to right	Ball of foot	2 or S
3	Step on RF	Body still turns to right	Ball of foot	1 or S
4	Step on LF	Body still turns to right	Toe	2 or S

Step	Feet Positions	Amount of Turn	Footwork	Timing
5	Step on RF	Body still turns to right	Toe	1 or S
6	Step on LF	Commence to turn body to left	Ball of foot	2 or S
7	Step on RF	Body still turns to left	Ball of foot	1 or S
8	Step on LF	Body still turns to left	Ball flat	2 or S

Repeat

Lady

Dances the normal opposite but as the gentleman is on the inside of the circle, the lady travels on the first half slightly leftwards and on the second half slightly rightwards.

Exits. Sur Place, Basic Movement.

Ecart et Véronique

This movement can be commenced facing wall, facing L.O.D., or facing diagonally to centre.

Entry. Sur Place.

Step	Feet Positions	Amount of Turn	Footwork	Timing
Gentleman				
1	Step on RF (Appel)	None	Ball flat	1 or S
2	LF forward	None	Heel flat	2 or S
3	RF to side	None	Ball flat	1 or S
4	LF crosses behind RF in Fallaway	⅛ turn to left	Ball flat	2 or S
5–12	Swivel on both feet finishing with weight on LF	⅜ turn to left	Feet flat, weight on ball of foot	1, 2, 1, 2, 1, 2, 1, 2 or S, S, S, S, S, S, S, S
13	RF forward	Curving to left	Ball of foot	1 or S
14	LF forward	Curving to left	Ball of foot	2 or S
15	RF forward	Curving to left	Ball of foot	1 or S
16	LF forward	Curving to left	Ball of foot	2 or S
17	RF forward	Curving to left having turned approximately ½ turn in last 5 steps	Ball of foot	1 or S

PASO DOBLE

18	LF crosses behind RF	Turning sharply approximately ¼ turn to left	Ball of foot	2 or S
19	RF closes to LF	None	Ball flat	1 or S
20	Mark time on LF	None	Ball flat	2 or S

Lady

1	Step on LF (Appel)	None	Ball flat	1 or S
2	RF back	None	Ball flat	2 or S
3	LF to side	None	Ball flat	1 or S
4	RF crosses behind LF in Fallaway	Approximately ¼ turn to right	Ball flat	2 or S
5	LF forward	Commencing to curve left	Heel flat	1 or S
6–12	Forward R, L, R, L, R, L, R	Curving approximately ¾ turn to left	All steps on ball of foot	2, 1, 2, 1, 2, 1, 2 or S, S, S, S, S, S
13	LF forward	Curving left	Ball of foot	1 or S
14	RF forward	Curving left	Ball of foot	2 or S
15	LF forward	Curving left	Ball of foot	1 or S
16	RF forward	Curving left	Ball of foot	2 or S
17	LF forward	Curving left having made approximately ½ turn in last 5 steps	Ball of foot	1 or S
18	RF closes or crosses to LF	Turning sharply approximately ¼ turn to left	Ball of foot	2 or S
19	Mark time on LF	None	Ball flat	1 or S
20	Mark time on RF	None	Ball flat	2 or S

Note. Between steps 5 and 8 the lady moves to gentleman's left side and remains in this position until step 17. Couple then revert to closed position on steps 18 to 20.

Exit. Sur Place.

The Banderillas

This figure pictures the action of the *torero* when he plants the *banderillas*—or hooked sticks—into the neck of the bull.

96 LATIN AND AMERICAN DANCES

Entry. Dance the fifteen steps of La Passe or seven steps of the Huit, and on the last step the gentleman leads the lady strongly across his body to his left side to a position left hip to left hip. He extends his left arm outwards to his left and holds his partner with his right hand close to her left elbow and dances as follows—

Step   Feet Positions   Amount of Turn   Footwork   Timing

Gentleman. Mark time for seven counts, 1, 2, 1, 2, 1, 2, 1, R, L, R, L, R, L, R. On step 8, count 2, take a long step to the side with LF moving to lady's right side into a position of right hip to right hip with right arm outstretched and left hand on lady's right elbow, then continue as follows—

Mark time for six counts, 1, 2, 1, 2, 1, 2, R, L, R, L, R, L, ball of foot on steps 1 to 14, except step 8 which is ball flat.

15	RF forward outside partner on her right side	None	Heel flat	1 or S
16	LF to side	None	Ball flat	2 or S
17	RF closes to LF	None	Ball flat	1 or S
18	Transfer weight on LF	None	Ball flat	2 or S

Lady. Mark time for 8 counts, 1, 2, 1, 2, 1, 2, 1, 2, L, R, L, R, L, R, L, R. Mark time for 6 counts, 1, 2, 1, 2, 1, 2, L, R, L, R, L, R, using ball of foot on each step.

15	LF back	None	Ball flat	1 or S
16	RF to side	None	Ball flat	2 or S
17	LF closes to RF	None	Ball flat	1 or S
18	Transfer weight to RF	None	Ball flat	2 or S

Exit. Sur Place, Basic Movement.

Syncopated Separation

Entry. Sur Place.

Step   Feet Positions   Amount of Turn   Footwork   Timing

Gentleman. This figure can be commenced facing L.O.D.

Entry. After first four steps of ordinary separation, but still holding partner with right hand, having extended right arm. Count 1, 2, 1, 2.

5	RF back loosely crossing behind LF	None	Ball of foot	1 or S

6	LF back loosely crossing behind RF	None	Ball of foot	2 or S
7	RF back loosely crossing behind LF	None	Ball of foot	1 or S
8	LF back loosely crossing behind RF	None	Ball flat	2
9	RF closes to LF	None	Ball flat	a
10	LF points to side without weight	None	Toe	1
11	LF closes to RF	None	Ball flat	a
12	RF points to side without weight	None	Toe	2 or S
13	RF crosses behind LF	⅛ turn to left	Ball flat	1 or ½ beat Q
14	LF to side	⅛ turn to left	Ball flat	"and" or ½ beat Q
15	RF crosses in front of LF	⅛ turn to left	Ball flat	2 or 1 beat S
16–19	Swivel on both feet finishing with weight on RF	½ turn to left	Feet flat, pressure on RF	1 or S 2 or S 1 or S 2 or S
20	LF forward in line with partner	None	Heel flat	1 or S
21	RF to side	Slight turn to left	Ball flat	2 or S
22	LF closes to RF	Slight turn to left	Ball flat	1 or S
23	Mark time on RF	None	Ball flat	2 or S

Note. On steps 8 to 11 the beat values are as follows: step 8, ¾ beat; step 9, ¼ beat; step 10, ¾ beat; step 11, ¼ beat.

Lady (backing L.O.D.)

5	LF forward crossing loosely in front of RF	None	Ball of foot	1 or S

Step	Feet Positions	Amount of Turn	Footwork	Timing
6	RF forward crossing loosely in front of LF	None	Ball of foot	2 or S
7	LF forward crossing loosely in front of RF	None	Ball of foot	1 or S
8	RF forward crossing loosely in front of LF	None	Ball flat	2
9	LF closes to RF	None	Ball flat	a
10	RF points to side without weight	None	Toe	1
11	RF closes to LF	None	Ball flat	a
12	LF points to side without weight	None	Toe	2 or S
13	LF forward and across in front of RF outside, partner on L side	$\frac{1}{8}$ turn to left	Ball flat	1 or $\frac{1}{2}$ beat Q
14	RF to side	$\frac{1}{8}$ turn to left	Ball flat	"and" or $\frac{1}{2}$ beat Q
15	LF back and slightly behind RF	$\frac{1}{8}$ turn to left	Ball of foot	2 or 1 beat S
16	RF to side in PP	$\frac{1}{4}$ turn to right	Ball of foot	1 or S
17	LF forward	Curving $\frac{1}{8}$ turn to left	Ball of foot	2 or S
18	RF forward	Curving $\frac{1}{8}$ turn to left	Ball of foot	1 or S
19	LF forward pivoting to left at the end of the step	Pivoting $\frac{1}{2}$ turn to left	Ball flat	2 or S
20	RF back	None	Ball flat	1 or S
21	LF to side	Slight turn to left	Ball flat	2 or S
22	RF closes to LF	None	Ball flat	1 or S
23	Mark time LF	None	Ball flat	2 or S

Exits. Basic Movement, Sur Place.

Note. On steps 8 to 11 the beat values are: step 8, $\frac{3}{4}$ beat; step 9, $\frac{1}{4}$ beat; step 10, $\frac{3}{4}$ beat; step 11, $\frac{1}{4}$ beat.

The Twists

This figure is usually commenced facing wall.

Entry. First four steps of the Sixteen, R, L, R, L, count 1, 2, 1, 2, or S, S, S, S.

Step	Feet Positions	Amount of Turn	Footwork	Timing
Gentleman				
5	RF crosses behind LF	½ turn to right	Ball flat	1 or S
6	RF forward on lady's right side	Commence to turn to right	Heel flat or ball flat	2 or S
7	LF to side	Continue to turn to right making ½ turn between steps 6 and 7	Ball flat	1 or S
8	RF crosses behind LF	½ turn to right	Ball flat	2 or S
9–10	Repeat steps 6 and 7	—	—	1, 2 or S, S
11	RF crosses behind LF	¼ turn to right	Ball flat	1 or S
12	Transfer weight on to RF close to LF	None	Ball flat	2 or S

Note. On steps 5, 8, 11 the gentleman turns sharply to R on the balls of both feet, finishing with weight on left foot.

Step	Feet Positions	Amount of Turn	Footwork	Timing
Lady				
5	LF forward outside partner on his right side	Commence to turn to right	Ball	1 or Q
"and"	RF forward outside partner	Continue to turn to right making ½ turn between steps 5 "and"	Ball	"and" or Q
6	LF back	Continue to turn to right	Ball heel	2 or S
7	RF nearly closes to LF	Continue to turn to right making ½ turn between steps 6 and 7	Heel ball	1 or S

Step	Feet Positions	Amount of Turn	Footwork	Timing
8	LF forward outside partner	Continue to turn to right	Ball	2 or Q
"and"	RF forward outside partner	Continue to turn to right making ½ turn between steps 8 "and"	Ball	"and" or Q
9–10	Repeat steps 6 and 7	—	—	1, 2 or S, S
11	LF forward outside partner	Continue to turn to right	Ball	1 or Q
"and"	RF forward outside partner	Continue to turn to right making ¼ turn between steps 11 "and"	Ball	"and" or Q
12	LF closes to RF	None	Ball flat	2 or S

Note. On steps 6 and 7 the lady dances a heel turn similar to the lady's heel turn in the Slow Foxtrot. The Twists should move along L.O.D. and be performed only when there is space as it is not a figure that can be easily condensed.

Exits. Sur Place, Coup de Pique, The Attack.

Amalgamation

Gentleman

Commence facing L.O.D. and with right foot.
Sur Place, four times, no turn.
Basic Step, forward four times, no turn.
Sur Place, four times, turning to left and finish backing wall.
Chassés to right, four times (eight steps) finish backing wall.
Sur Place, four times, turning to right and finish facing L.O.D.
Déplacement, finish facing centre.
Sur Place, four times turning to left, finish backing L.O.D.
Basic Step, back four times, finish backing L.O.D.
Sur Place, six times turning to left, finish facing L.O.D.
Separation, with variation, finish backing wall.

Sur Place, six times turning to left, finish facing wall.
Sixteen, commence facing wall, finish backing wall.
Sur Place, four times turning to right, finish facing L.O.D.

Repeat from beginning.

Note. Again as in the Samba this amalgamation would fit a fairly long room. For a smaller room, either more or less turning Sur Place could be employed to enable the dancers to move around the room.

Lady
Normal opposite.

PASO DOBLE VARIATIONS

The Coup de Pique

Entry. Sur Place.

Step	Feet Positions	Amount of Turn	Footwork	Timing
Gentleman				
1	RF points across LF without weight	¼ turn to left	Toe	1 or S
2	RF closes to LF	¼ turn to right	Ball flat	2 or S
3	LF back	¼ turn to left	Ball flat	1 or S
4	RF closes to LF	¼ turn to right	Ball flat	2 or S
Lady				
1	LF points across RF without weight	¼ turn to right	Toe	1 or S
2	LF closes to RF	¼ turn to left	Ball flat	2 or S
3	RF back	¼ turn to right	Ball flat	1 or S
4	LF closes to RF	¼ turn to left	Ball flat	2 or S

Note. Step 1 symbolizes the thrust of a sword and step 3 a rapid withdrawal after the thrust.

The following five figures have been added to the syllabus of the I.S.T.D. and I will briefly describe them.

Step	Feet Positions	Amount of Turn	Timing
5	Repeat step 3	¼ turn to left	1
6	RF to side	¼ turn to right	2
7	LF closes to RF	No turn	and
8	RF to side	No turn	1
9	LF closes to RF	No turn	2

Lady dances the same steps as man but when he is on his RF she is on her LF and vice versa.

102 LATIN AND AMERICAN DANCES

Open Telemark

Usually commenced facing D.C.

Entry. Sur Place.

Step	Feet Positions	Amount of Turn	Count	Timing
Gentleman				
1	Slip Appel RF, lady LF	⅛ to left	1	1
2	LF forward, lady RF back	Continue to turn	2	2
3	RF to side, lady left heel closes to right heel	Continue to turn	3	1
4	LF to side in PP, lady forward in PP	Continue to turn	4	2
5	RF forward and across in PP, lady LF forward in PP	Continue to turn	5	1
6	LF closes to RF, lady RF closes to LF	Having completed ⅞ turn to left	6	2
7	RF to side, lady LF to side	None	7	1
8	LF closes to RF, lady RF closes to LF	None	8	2

Footwork. *Man* BF, HF, BF, BF, HF, BF, BF, BF. *Lady* BF, BF, WF, HF, HF, BF, BF, BF.

Exits. Sur Place, Sixteen, Elevations, Separations.

Fallaway Reverse

This figure usually commenced facing diagonal to centre on L.O.D.

Entry. Sur Place.

Step	Feet Positions	Amount of Turn	Count	Timing
Gentleman				
1	Slip Appel RF, lady LF	⅛ to left	1	1
2	LF forward, lady RF back	Continue turn to left	2	2
3	RF to side and slightly back, lady LF to side and slightly forward	Continue turn to left	3	1

PASO DOBLE 103

Step	Feet Positions	Amount of Turn	Count	Timing
4	LF back in Fallaway, lady RF back in Fallaway	Continue turn to left	4	2
5	RF back, lady pivot on RF, then LF forward	Continue turn to left	5	1
6	Replace weight forward to LF, lady back RF and slightly towards right	Completing ⅞ turn to left	6	2
7	RF to side, lady LF to side	None	7	1
8	LF closes to RF, lady RF closes to LF	None	8	2

Footwork. *Man* BF, HF, BF, BF, BF, HF, BF, BF.
Lady BF, BF, BF, BF, B(RF), BF(LF), BF, BF, BF.

Exits. Sur Place, Elevation, Sixteen, Separation.

Chassé Cape

Usually commenced facing wall.
Entry. Sur Place.

Step	Feet Positions	Amount of Turn	Count	Timing
Gentleman				
1–4	As 1–4 of the sixteen	As 1–4 sixteen	1, 2, 3, 4	1, 2, 1, 2
5	RF back, lady LF forward	Continue to turn right	5	1
6	LF back outside partner on right side, lady LF forward	Completing ⅜ turn right	6	2
7	RF forward outside partner on right side, lady LF closes to RF	Continue to turn right	7	1
8	LF to side, lady RF to side	Completing ⅜ turn right	8	2
9	RF closes to LF lady LF closes to RF	None	and	and
10	LF to side, lady RF to side	⅛ turn to right	1	2
11	RF back partner outside on left side, lady LF forward	¼ turn to left	2	1

104 LATIN AND AMERICAN DANCES

Step	Feet Positions	Amount of Turn	Count	Timing
12	LF forward outside partner on left side, lady RF closes to LF	Continue to turn left	3	1
13	RF to side, lady LF to side	Completing ⅜ to left	4	2
14	LF closes to RF, lady RF closes to LF	None	and	and
15	RF to side, lady LF to side	⅛ turn to left	5	1
16	LF back partner outside on right side, lady RF forward	¼ turn to right	6	2
17, 18, 19, 20, 21, 22	Repeat steps 7, 8, 9, 10, 11, 12		7, 8 and 1, 2, 3	1, 2 and 1, 2, 1
23	RF forward, lady LF forward in left side by side position, man releasing hold with his right hand now both facing L.O.D.	—		
24	LF forward lady, RF forward (pressure step without full weight) and man's left arm and lady's right arm raised	None	5	1
25, 26, 27	Hold position for 3 counts *Exit*	None	6, 7, 8	2, 1, 2
28, 29, 30	Close LF to RF turning left to face partner at the same time, turning lady to her right for approx. 1½ turns, RLR This can be followed by a Chassé to side	—	12 1 and 2 34	12 1 and 2 12

Travelling Spins from Promenade Position

Usually commenced facing wall.
Entry. Sur Place.

Step	Feet Positions	Amount of Turn	Count	Timing
Gentleman				
1	Appel on RF	None	1	1
2	LF to side in PP	⅛ to left	2	2
3	RF forward and across	None	3	1
4	LF to side	None	4	2
5–8	Repeat steps 3 and 4 twice	—	5, 6, 7, 8	1, 2, 1, 2

Footwork. WF on step 1, WF on BF on steps 2–8.

Note. On step 2 release hold with right hand raise lady's right arm and lead her to make 3 turns to her right on steps 3–8.

Exit

| 1 | RF forward and across, lady LF forward and across | — | 1 | 1 |
| 2 | LF closes to RF, lady RF closes to LF | — | 2 | 2 |

Travelling Spins from Counter Promenade

Gentleman and lady dance the same steps as described on page 90, but on step 5 he releases hold with his right hand and raises her right arm and leads her to turn for approx. 1¾ turns to her right, on steps 5, 6, 7 and 8.

Exit

| 1 | RF forward and across, lady LF forward and across | — | 1 | 1 |
| 2 | LF closes to RF, lady RF closes to LF | — | 2 | 2 |

EXAMINATION QUESTIONS AND ANSWERS

Paso Doble for Associates

Basic Movement or Sur Place

Q. Are the heels raised?

A. No, it is better if the heels lightly brush the floor.

Q. Are the knees straight?

A. No, they are slightly relaxed but the body is very upright.

Elevation

Q. Describe the Elevation.

A. The Elevation is a series of steps stretching the body from the ankle followed by a series of steps relaxing the knees but not the body.

Déplacement

Q. Is there a heel lead in the Déplacement?

A. A heel lead is used on steps 1 and 2 but if turning on the third step, then it is ball flat on steps 3 and 4.

The Sixteen

Q. Is the sixteen danced in close contact?

A. No, about six inches apart. If it is danced in close contact the lady cannot dance steps 4, 5 and 6 correctly.

Separation

Q. Describe the lady's deportment.

A. Her deportment is upright with the left arm held naturally and just lower than her left shoulder.

Appel

Q. Is this movement a stamp on the floor?

A. Definitely not, it is just a firm step taken on the spot.

Huit

Q. What does the lady represent in this figure?

A. She represents the cape which the *torero* is waving from his left side to his right side then back again to his left.

Members' and Fellows' Syllabus

The Promenades

Q. On which steps does the gentleman loosen his hold with his right hand?

A. On steps 4, 5, 6, 7, 8, to enable himself and his partner to use marching steps.

La Passe

Q. Are steps 7, 10 and 13 ball flat or heel flat?

A. Either, but the steps must be firm and when the step is taken forward, i.e. on the RF, the LF must remain in place for three counts.

Syncopated Separation

Q. What is the beat value in 2/4 time?

A. Up to the first seven steps, 1 beat on each step, $\frac{3}{4}$ beat on step 8, $\frac{1}{4}$ beat on step 9, $\frac{3}{4}$ beat on step 10, $\frac{1}{4}$ beat on step 11, 1 beat on step 12, $\frac{1}{2}$ beat on step 13, $\frac{1}{2}$ beat on step 14, 1 beat on steps 15, 16, 17, 18, 19, 20, 21, 22, and 23.

Ecart et Véronique

Q. Are the walking forward steps, as lady, all danced on the ball of the foot?

A. No, the first one which is step 5 has a heel lead with knee very relaxed. The others are on the ball of the foot.

Banderillas

Q. Are arm movements necessary?

A. Yes, the figure represents the matador sticking the *banderillas* into the skin of the bull, therefore the extended arms are lower than the other arms which are held with the elbows rather high.

The Twists

Q. Is a very strong lead required?

A. Yes, especially when the gentleman crosses his RF behind his LF, he "whips" the lady round on his right side; this lead is given mainly with his right hand.

The Whip & Points.
Stop & Go.
Spanish Arms.

SECTION IV

THE AMERICAN JIVE

This dance has been called by many titles—Jitterbug, Lindy, Jive or Swing—but call it what you like it is a wonderful way to interpret the swing music. No other steps could fit so perfectly. The Jive gained in popularity during the last war in many parts of the world. Wherever there were G.I.s there was Jive and when they returned to America they left this legacy behind them. The Jive can be danced in two styles, the Double Lindy and the Triple Lindy. The last named is the most popular in America and this is the one I will describe in this book.

Many new dances have come to us from America since the war—the most famous being the Twist. The new dances come and go, but the Jive stays, perhaps because it has definite basic steps. Although I learned the Jive in England, whenever I visit America and dance the Jive I find I can follow any partner because the basic steps are exactly the same as we have here. This is not surprising as every step we do has been learned from Americans!

JIVE (The American Swing)

Tempo. 40–46 bars per minute.

Musical Timing. 4/4—four counts to each bar of music.

Hold. Slightly apart as in Rumba.

THE AMERICAN JIVE

The footwork of the Jive is affected appreciably by individual interpretation and speed of music, therefore the footwork is given as a guide.

The Jive Chassé can be commenced on either RF or LF and is counted 3 a 4, which has a beat value of $\frac{3}{4}$ beat, $\frac{1}{4}$ beat, whole beat.

Basic Movement

Entries. Basic Movement in Fallaway, Link.

Step	Feet Positions	Amount of Turn	Timing
Gentleman			
1	Step on RF	None	1
2	Step on LF about 6 inches to side	None	2
3	Step on RF moving it 2 or 3 inches to side	None	3
4	Move LF about 2 or 3 inches towards RF	None	a
5	Small step to side on RF	None	4

Lady

Normal opposite.

Footwork. Ball of foot or ball flat on each step.

The Rock Basic

Note. An alternative basic movement may be commenced on the LF, using two Jive chassés, counted 1, 2, 3 and 4, 3 and 4. The last three steps of the Basic Movement are known as a jive chassé.

Exits. Basic Movement in Fallaway.

Basic Movement in Fallaway

Entries. Basic Movement, Whip.

Step	Feet Positions	Amount of Turn	Timing
Gentleman			
1	LF back leaving RF in place.	⅛ turn to left	1
2	Replace weight on RF	⅛ turn to right	2
3	Step on LF to side	None	3
4	Draw RF about 2 or 3 inches towards LF	None	a
5	Move LF about 2 or 3 inches to side	None	4

Lady

Normal opposite except on step 1 turns ¼ to R on step 2 ¼ to L.

Footwork. Ball of foot or ball flat on each step.

Exits. Basic Movement, Promenade Walk, Whip.

Note. This figure can be danced with an additional Jive chassé to right, counted 1, 2, 3 and 4, 3 and 4. Lady normal opposite.

Basic Throwaway

Entries. Basic Movement in Fallaway, Link.

Step	Feet Positions	Amount of Turn	Timing
Gentleman			
1	Step on RF	None	1
2	Step on LF about 6 inches to side	None	2
3	RF to side releasing lady with right hand	⅛ turn to right, between steps 3 and 5	3

THE AMERICAN JIVE

4	Draw LF towards RF	—	a
5	RF to side	—	4

Lady

1	Step on LF	None	1
2	Step on RF	None	2
3	LF to side	⅛ turn to left	3
4	Draw RF towards LF	between steps 3 and 5	a
5	LF to side	—	4

Footwork. Ball of foot or ball flat on each step.

Exit. Link.

The Link

Entries. Throwaway, Change of Places Left to Right, Throwaway Whip.

Step   Feet Positions   Amount of Turn   Timing

Gentleman (commences in open position, finishes in normal closed hold)

1	LF back leaving RF in place	None	1
2	Replace weight on RF	None	2
3	LF forward regaining normal hold	None	3
4	Draw RF towards LF 2 or 3 inches	None	a
5	LF forward	None	4

Footwork. Ball of foot or ball flat on each step.

Lady

1	RF back leaving LF in place	None	1
2	Replace weight on LF	None	2

Step	Feet Positions	Amount of Turn	Timing
3	RF forward	None	3
4	Draw LF towards RF 2 or 3 inches	None	a
5	RF forward	None	4

Footwork. Ball of foot or ball flat on each step.
Exits. Basic Movement, Whip.
Note. This figure can be danced with an additional Jive chassé to right, counted 1, 2, 3 a 4, 3 a 4. Lady normal opposite. This figure is called Link Rock.

If the lady has travelled well away from her partner on the second 3 a 4 of the Change of Places Left to Right, she would close RF to LF on step 1 of the link and take a step forward RF on step 2, the footwork on step 2 would then be heel flat. This must be treated as an alternative to the Link described above.

The Whip

Entries. Link, Promenade Walks, Basic Movement in Fallaway.

Step	Feet Positions	Amount of Turn	Timing

Gentleman

1	RF crosses behind LF	$\frac{1}{4}$ turn to right	1
2	LF to side	$\frac{1}{4}$ turn to right	2
3	RF to side	$\frac{1}{8}$ turn to right	3
4	Draw LF towards RF	between steps 3 and 5	"and"
5	RF to side	—	4

Note. More turn can be made on this figure. Minimum as given above and maximum one and one-eighth turns to right. The extra turn is usually made on steps 1 and 2.

Footwork. Ball of foot or ball flat on each step.

THE AMERICAN JIVE 113

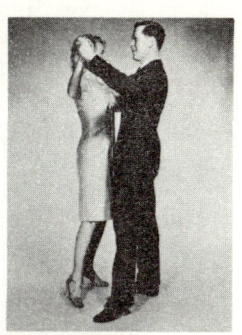

Jive—The Whip
Steps 1–3
Steps 4 and 5

Lady

1	LF forward	Approximately ¼ turn to right	1
2	RF forward outside partner	Approximately ¼ turn to right	2
3	LF to side	⅜ turn to right	3
4	Draw RF towards LF	between steps 3 and 5	a
5	LF to side	—	4

Note. More turn can be made on this figure. Minimum

as given above and maximum one and three-eighths turns to right. The extra turn is usually made on steps 1 a 2.

Footwork. Ball of foot or ball flat on each step.

Exits. Change of Places Right to Left, Basic Movement in Fallaway, Curly Whip.

Change of Places Right to Left

Entries. Basic Movement, Whip, Promenade Walks.

Step	Feet Positions	Amount of Turn	Timing
Gentleman			
1	LF back leaving RF in place	⅛ turn to left	1
2	Replace weight on RF	None	2
3	LF forward	None	3
4	Draw RF to LF 2 or 3 inches	None	a
5	LF forward releasing lady with R hand	⅛ turn to left	4
6	RF forward	None	3
7	Draw LF to RF 2 or 3 inches	None	a
8	RF forward	None	4

Footwork. Ball of foot or ball flat on each step.

Lady			
1	RF back leaving LF in place	¼ turn to right	1
2	Replace weight on LF	¼ turn to left between steps	2
3	RF to side	2 and 3	3
4	Draw LF towards RF 2 or 3 inches	None	a
5	RF to side	¾ turn to right	4
6	LF to side	between steps	3

THE AMERICAN JIVE

7	Draw RF towards LF 2 or 3 inches	5 and 8	a
8	LF back, and slightly to side	—	4

Footwork. Ball of foot or ball flat on each step.

Exits. Change of Places Left to Right, American Spin, Stop and Go.

Note. On steps 6 to 8 lady passes under raised arms.

Change of Places Left to Right

Entries. Change of Places Right to Left, American Spin Change of Places behind Back, Throwaway Whip.

Step	Feet Positions	Amount of Turn	Timing
Gentleman			
1	LF back leaving RF in place	None	1
2	Replace weight on RF		2
3	LF to side	¼ turn to right	3
4	Draw RF towards LF 2 or 3 inches	between steps 2 and 5	a
5	LF to side	—	4
6	RF forward	None	3
7	Draw LF towards RF 2 or 3 inches	None	a
8	RF forward	None	4
Lady			
1	RF back leaving LF in place	None	1
2	Replace weight on LF	¾ turn to left between steps	2
3	RF to side	2 and 6	3
4	Draw LF towards RF 2 or 3 inches	—	a
5	RF back	—	4

JIVE—CHANGE OF PLACES RIGHT TO LEFT
Steps 1, 2
Steps 5, 6

JIVE—CHANGE OF PLACES RIGHT TO LEFT
  Steps 3, 4
  Steps 7, 8

Step	Feet Positions	Amount of Turn	Timing
6	LF back	—	3
7	Draw RF towards LF 2 or 3 inches	None	a
8	LF back	None	4

Footwork. Ball of foot or ball flat on each step.

Exits. Change of Hands behind Back, Link, American Spin, Windmill, Spanish Arms, Single Spin.

Note. On steps 3–5 lady passes under raised arms.

Promenade Walks

Entries. Basic Movement, or Alternative Basic Movement when commenced with LF.

Step	Feet Positions	Amount of Turn	Timing
Gentleman			
1	LF back leaving RF in place	$\frac{1}{8}$ turn to left	1
2	Replace weight on RF	None	2
3	LF forward	None	3
4	Draw RF 2 or 3 inches towards LF	None	a
5	LF forward	None	4
6	RF forward	None	3
7	Draw LF towards RF 2 or 3 inches	None	a
8	RF forward	None	4
Repeat steps 3 to 8			

Footwork. Ball of foot or ball flat on each step.

Lady			
1	RF back leaving LF in place	$\frac{1}{4}$ turn to right	1
2	Replace weight forward on LF	$\frac{1}{4}$ turn to left between steps	2
3	RF to side	2 and 3	3
4	Draw LF towards RF 2 or 3 inches	None	a

5	RF to side	¼ turn to right	4
6	LF forward	between steps 5 and 6	3
7	Draw RF towards LF 2 or 3 inches	None	a
8	LF forward	Commence to turn to left	4

Repeat steps 1 to 8

Footwork. Ball of foot or ball flat on each step.

Exits. Alternative Basic Movement, last three steps of Change of Places Right to Left, Whip.

Change of Hands Behind Back

Entries. Throwaway, Change of Places Left to Right.

Step	Feet Positions	Amount of Turn	Timing
Gentleman			
1	LF back leaving RF in place	A gradual turn is made to left approximately ½ turn between steps 1 and 8	1
2	Replace weight on RF		2
3	LF forward changing lady's hand into R hand		3
4	Draw RF towards LF 2 or 3 inches	—	a
5	LF forward	—	4
6	RF to side changing lady's hand into L hand behind back	—	3
7	Draw LF back towards RF 2 or 3 inches	—	a
8	RF back and slightly to side		4

Footwork. Ball of foot or ball flat on each step.

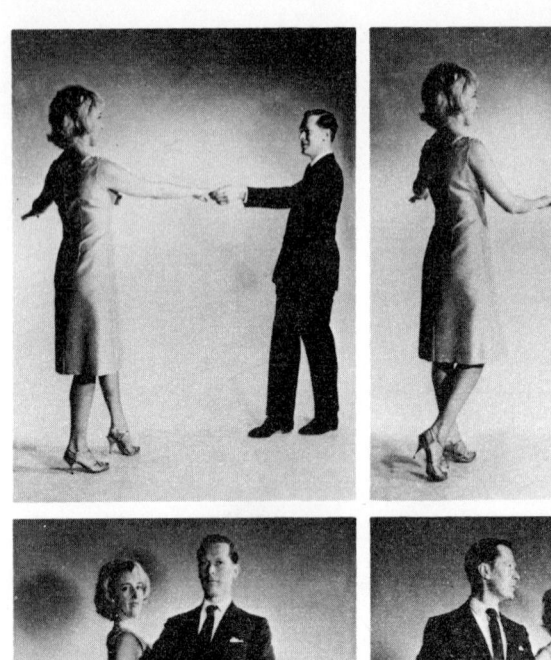

JIVE—CHANGE OF HANDS BEHIND BACK
Steps 1, 2
Steps 5, 6

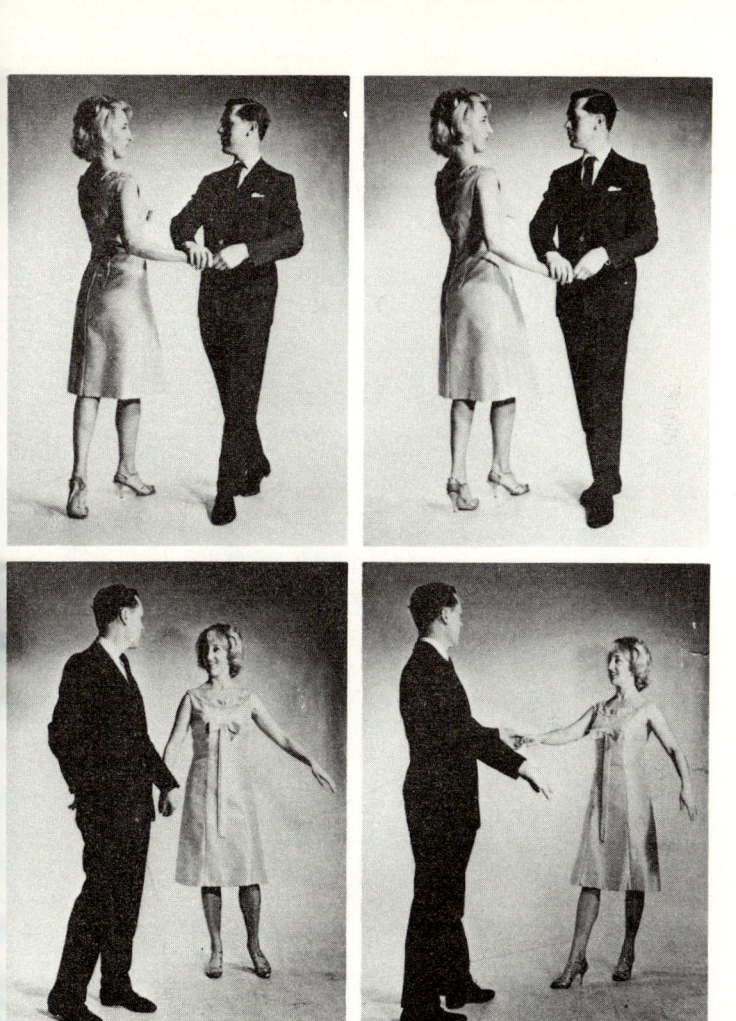

JIVE—CHANGE OF HANDS BEHIND BACK
  Steps 3, 4
  Steps 7, 8

122   LATIN AND AMERICAN DANCES

Step	Feet Positions	Amount of Turn	Timing
Lady			
1	RF back leaving LF in place	A gradual turn is made to right making approximately ½ turn between steps 1 and 8	1
2	Replace weight on LF		2
3	RF forward		3
4	Draw LF towards RF 2 or 3 inches		a
5	RF forward	—	4
6	LF to side	—	3
7	Draw RF towards LF 2 or 3 inches	—	a
8	LF back and slightly to side	—	4

Footwork. Ball of foot or ball flat on each step.

Exits. Change of Places Left to Right.

American Spin

Entries. Change of Places Right to Left changing hands, finishing gentleman's R holding lady's R hand.

Step	Feet Positions	Amount of Turn	Timing
Gentleman			
1	LF back leaving RF in place	None	1
2	Replace weight on RF	None	2
3	LF to side small step	None	3
4	Transfer weight to RF	None	a
5	Transfer weight to LF, releasing lady	None	4
6	Transfer weight to RF	None	3
7	Transfer weight to LF	None	a

THE AMERICAN JIVE

8	Transfer weight to RF regaining hold with R hand	None	4

Footwork. Ball of foot or ball flat on each step.

Note. On step 5 the lady and gentleman brace their right hand and arm. He gives her a slight push forward with his right hand and as the lady's right hand and arm are braced it gives her the necessary impetus to turn. He releases her and regains hold on step 8, when he can repeat the 8 steps once or twice.

Lady

1	RF back leaving LF in place	None	1
2	Replace weight on LF	None	2
3	RF forward	None	3
4	Draw LF towards RF 2 or 3 inches	None	a
5	RF forward	Full turn to right between steps 5 and 8	4
6	LF to side		3
7	Transfer weight to RF close to LF		a
8	Transfer weight to LF	—	4

Footwork. Ball of foot or ball flat on each step except step 5 which is ball of foot.

Exits. Change of Places Left to Right changing hands on step 8.

Note. This figure can be danced preceded by Change of Places Left to Right without changing hands. The lady's turn, steps 5–8, is danced under her right and the gentleman's left arm.

Simple Spin

Entry. Change of Places Left to Right, L, R, L, R, L, R, L, R, 1, 2, 3 a 4, 3 a 4 slightly overturning to R about $\frac{1}{8}$ turn.

JIVE—AMERICAN SPIN
Steps 1, 2
Steps 5, 6

JIVE—AMERICAN SPIN
   Steps 3, 4
   Steps 7, 8

Note. The lead in the last three steps is important and can be described as follows—

The gentleman who is holding the lady's right hand in his left hand leads her normally under his left arm for the first count of 3 a 4; on the second count of 3 a 4, he lowers his arm to about waist level keeping the lady closer to him and pulling his forearm across his body so that his left hand moves towards his right side. He now gently pushes the lady's right hand with his left hand to initiate her spinning movement and releases her right hand to allow her to complete her spin. His steps are as follows—

Step	*Feet Positions*	*Amount of Turn*	*Timing*
1	Step on LF	¼ turn to L	1
2	Step on RF	None	2

The footwork is ball of foot or ball flat on each step.

Lady

1	Step on RF	½ turn to R	1
2	Side on LF	½ turn to R	2

Note. When the lady has finished her change of places left to right she is facing the gentleman. As she spins to right she keeps her feet slightly apart and when she has completed her two half turns she is again facing the gentleman.

Footwork. Ball of foot or ball flat on each step.

Exit. Change of Places Left to Right.

Fallaway Throwaway

Entry. Basic Movement.

Step	*Feet Positions*	*Amount of Turn*	*Timing*
Gentleman			
1–5	As 5 steps of Basic Movement in Fallaway, releasing lady with R hand	⅛ turn to left on step 1	1, 2, 3 and 4
6	RF forward	⅛ turn to left	3

THE AMERICAN JIVE

| 7 | Draw LF 2 or 3 inches towards RF | — | a |
| 8 | RF forward | — | 4 |

Lady

1–5	As 5 steps of Basic Movement in Fallaway	¼ turn to right on step 1, ¼ turn left between steps 2 and 5	1, 2, 3 a 4
6	LF back	Up to ¼ turn to left between steps 6 and 8	3
7	Draw RF 2 or 3 inches towards LF		a
8	LF back	—	4

Footwork. Ball of foot or ball flat on each step.
Exits. Link, Chicken Walk.

Whip Throwaway

Entries. Link, Promenade Walk, Basic Movement in Fallaway.

Step	Feet Positions	Amount of Turn	Timing
Gentleman			
1	RF crosses behind LF	¼ turn to right	1
2	LF to side, releasing lady with R hand	¼ turn to right	2
3	Transfer weight to RF	¼ turn to right between steps 3 and 5	3 a
4	Transfer weight to LF		
5	Transfer weight to RF	—	4

Footwork. Ball of foot or ball flat on each step.

Lady

| 1 | LF forward | ¼ turn to right | 1 |

Step	Feet Positions	Amount of Turn	Timing
2	RF forward outside partner	¼ turn to right	2
3	LF to side	⅛ turn to right	3
4	Draw RF towards LF 2 or 3 inches	between steps 3 and 5	a
5	LF to side	—	4

Footwork. Ball of foot or ball flat on each step.
Exits. Change of Places Left to Right, Link.
Note. More turn can be made on this figure; the extra turn is usually made on steps 1 and 2.

Stop and Go / Traffic Lights

Entries. Change of Places Right to Left.

Step	Feet Positions	Amount of Turn	Timing
Gentleman			
1	LF back leaving RF in place	None	1
2	Replace weight on RF	None	2
3	LF forward	None	3
4	Draw RF towards LF 2 or 3 inches	None	a
5	LF forward	None	4
6	RF forward leaving LF in place	None	1
7	Replace weight on LF	None	2
8	RF back	None	3
9	Draw LF towards RF 2 or 3 inches	None	a
10	RF back	None	4

Footwork. Ball of foot or ball flat on each step.

Note. On step 5, the gentleman places his right hand on the lady's back to stop her movement. On step 7 he leads her with his right hand forward. On step 8 releases her with right hand.

Lady

1	RF back	None	1
2	Replace weight on LF	½ turn to left between steps	2
3	RF to side and slightly back	2 and 5	3
4	Draw LF towards RF 2 or 3 inches	—	a
5	RF back and slightly to side	—	4
6	LF back	None	1
7	Replace weight on RF	½ turn to right between steps	2
8	LF to side	7 and 10	3
9	Draw RF towards LF 2 or 3 inches	—	a
10	LF back and slightly to side	—	4

Footwork. Ball of foot or ball flat on each step.

Exits. Change of Places Left to Right.

The Spanish Arms

Entries. Change of Places Left to Right, finishing with gentleman's right hand holding lady's left hand, and his left hand holding her right hand.

Step	Feet Positions	Amount of Turn	Timing
Gentleman			
1	LF back, leaving RF in place	None	1
2	Replace weight on RF	¼ turn to right between steps	2

Step	Feet Positions	Amount of Turn	Timing
3	LF to side and slightly forward	2 and 5	3
4	Draw RF towards LF 2 or 3 inches	—	a
5	LF to side and slightly forward	—	4
6	RF forward	$\frac{1}{8}$ turn to right between steps	3
7	Draw LF towards RF 2 or 3 inches	6 and 8	a
8	RF forward	—	4

Footwork. Ball of foot or ball flat on each step.

Note. On steps 3, 4, 5 the gentleman raises his left arm over lady's head, still holding her right hand and holding her left hand in his right hand which is around her waist and both facing the same way. On steps 6, 7, 8 he leads her with both hands to turn and move away from him.

Lady

1	RF back leaving LF in place	None	1
2	Replace weight on LF	Approximately $\frac{1}{4}$ turn to left	2
3	RF to side	between steps	3
4	Draw LF towards RF 2 or 3 inches	2 and 5	a
5	RF to side	—	4
6	LF to side	Approximately	3
7	Draw RF towards LF 2 or 3 inches	$\frac{5}{8}$ turn to right between steps 6 and 8	a
8	LF back	—	4

Footwork. Ball of foot or ball flat on each step.

Exits. Change of Places Left to Right or the lady turning one and a half turns to right between steps 6 and 8, this is led by the gentleman raising his left hand, having released the lady with his right hand.

The Windmill Step

Entries. Change of Places Left to Right, finishing with gentleman's right hand holding lady's left hand, and left hand holding her right hand.

Step	Feet Positions	Amount of Turn	Timing
Gentleman			
1	LF back leaving RF in place	None	1
2	Replace weight on RF	$\frac{1}{4}$ turn to left between steps 2 and 5	2
3	LF forward (small step)		3
4	Draw RF towards LF 2 or 3 inches	—	a
5	LF forward	—	4
6	RF to side and slightly forward	$\frac{1}{8}$ turn to left between steps 6 and 8	3
7	Draw LF towards RF 2 or 3 inches		a
8	RF forward		4

Footwork. Ball of foot or ball flat on each step.

Note. On steps 3, 4, 5 the gentleman brings his partner close to him with arms outstretched, body inclining slightly to left.

On steps 6, 7, 8 he leads his partner to move back away from him, body inclining slightly to right.

Lady			
1	RF back leaving LF in place	None	1

Step	Feet Positions	Amount of Turn	Timing
2	Replace weight on LF	¼ turn to left between steps	2
3	RF forward	2 and 5	3
4	Draw LF towards RF 2 or 3 inches	—	a
5	RF forward	—	4
6	LF back	⅛ turn to left between steps 6 and 8	3
7	Draw RF towards LF 2 or 3 inches		a
8	LF back	—	4

Footwork. Ball of foot or ball flat on each step.

Exits. Change of Places Left to Right, having released lady with his right hand or Rolling off the Arm, having released lady with his left hand.

Rolling off the Arm

Entries. Change of Places Right to Left Changing Hands, Windmill.

Step	Feet Positions	Amount of Turn	Timing
Gentleman			
1	LF back leaving RF in place	None	1
2	Replace weight on RF	¼ turn to right between steps	2
3	LF to side and slightly forward	2 and 5	3
4	Draw RF towards LF 2 or 3 inches	—	a
5	LF to side and slightly forward	—	4
6	RF forward	¼ turn to right	1
7	LF forward	¼ turn to right	2
8	RF forward and slightly to side	⅛ turn to right between steps	3

THE AMERICAN JIVE

| 9 | Draw LF towards RF 2 or 3 inches | 8 and 10 | a |
| 10 | RF forward and slightly to side | — | 4 |

Note. When the figure is preceded by Change of Places Right to Left changing hands, and finishing with right hand in right hand, on steps 3, 4, 5 the gentleman leads the lady with his right hand to turn to left into the crook of his right arm, but if it is preceded by the Windmill he releases her right hand and leads her into the crook of his right arm, holding her left hand in his right.

Footwork. Ball of foot or ball flat on each step

Lady

1	RF back leaving LF in place	None	1
2	Replace weight on LF	¼ turn to left between steps	2
3	RF to side	2 and 5	3
4	Draw LF towards RF 2 or 3 inches	—	a
5	RF to side	—	4
6	LF back	¼ turn to right	1
7	RF back	¼ turn to right	2
8	LF to side	⅝ turn to right	3
9	Draw RF towards LF 2 or 3 inches	between steps 8 and 10	a
10	LF to side and slightly back	—	4

Footwork. Ball of foot or ball flat on each step.

Exits. Change of Places Left to Right Changing Hands, American Spin.

Curly Whip

Entry. Whip.

Step	Feet Positions	Amount of Turn	Timing
Gentleman			
1	LF forward	None	1
2	Replace weight on RF	½ turn to right between steps 2 and 5	2
3	LF to side		3
4	Move RF towards LF 2 or 3 inches	—	a
5	Replace weight on LF		4

Note. On step 1 the gentleman gently pushes his partner back, bringing her forward on step 2 and turning her under his raised left arm; but not entirely releasing her with his right hand on steps 3, 4, 5.

Footwork. Ball of foot or ball flat on each step.

Lady			
1	RF back	None	1
2	Replace weight on LF	½ turn to left between steps 2 and 5	2
3	RF to side		3
4	Move LF about 2 or 3 inches towards RF	—	a
5	Replace weight on RF	—	4

Footwork. Ball of foot or ball flat on each step.

Exit. Whip.

Chicken Walks

Entries. Fallaway Throwaway.

Step	Feet Positions	Amount of Turn	Timing
Gentleman			
1	LF back	None	1

THE AMERICAN JIVE 135

2	RF back	None	2
3	LF back	None	3
4	RF back	None	4

Footwork. Ball flat on each step.

Note. As gentleman takes his four short steps back holding his partner's right hand in his left hand, he gently pulls her forward.

Lady

1	RF forward toe turned out	None	1
2	LF forward toe turned out	None	2
3	RF forward toe turned out	None	3
4	LF forward toe turned out	None	4

Footwork. Heel flat on each step.

Note. As the lady steps forward on each step she leans back. When stepping forward with the RF she swivels slightly to the right and to the left when stepping with the left foot and vice versa, the swivel being made on the supporting foot.

Exit. Steps 3–8 of Fallaway Throwaway.

Amalgamation

Gentleman

Commence facing wall and with right foot.
Basic Movement, facing wall.
Basic Movement in Fallaway, facing wall.
Basic Throwaway, facing wall.
Link, facing wall.
Basic Movement, facing wall.
Change of Places R to L, finish facing L.O.D.
Change of Places L to R, finish facing wall.
Change of Hands Behind Back, finish backing wall.
Change of Places L to R, finish facing L.O.D.
Link, facing L.O.D.

Basic Step, facing L.O.D.

Change of Places R to L, with change of hands, finish backing wall.

American Spin, twice, backing wall.

Change of Places L to R, changing hands, finishing facing L.O.D.

Repeat from beginning.

Lady

Normal opposite.

JIVE VARIATIONS

Kicking Through (*see pages* 138–9)

Entry. Whip.

Step	Feet Positions	Amount of Turn	Timing
1	LF back in Fallaway	None	1
2	Replace weight on RF	None	2
3	Flick LF forward	None	3
4	Close LF to RF	¼ turn to right	4
5	Flick RF forward on partner's left side	None	1
6	RF closes to LF	None	2
7	Flick LF forward, between partner's feet	None	3
8	Close LF to RF	¼ turn to left	4
9	Flick RF forward	None	1
10	Close RF to LF	None	2

These ten steps can be repeated.

Exit. Fallaway Throwaway.

The lady's steps are the same as the gentleman's except when he turns R she turns L and vice versa. When he is on his LF she is on her RF and vice versa; she kicks between his feet on step 5 and on his left side on step 7.

Note. The type of step is for advanced dancers and should then only be used occasionally. It is essential that the

THE AMERICAN JIVE

knees are kept relaxed throughout the movement and when "flicking" the foot it is only raised a few inches from the floor.

Footwork. Ball of foot or ball flat on each step except when the flicking action is used. To get the correct action for this movement the lady and gentleman must feel that they are trying to shake their slipper from their foot.

The Catapult

Step　　　*Feet Positions*　　　*Amount of Turn*　　*Timing*

Gentleman. Dance Change of Places Right to Left and then Left to Right changing lady's right hand into gentleman's right hand.

1	LF back	None	1
2	Replace weight on RF	None	2
3, 4, 5	Jive chassé moving slightly forward, and raising right arm and turning the lady to left	None	3 a 4
6, 7, 8	Jive chassé to right, lady is now behind her partner and he has taken her left hand in his left hand	None	3 a 4
9	LF forward	None	1
10	Replace weight on RF releasing lady with R hand	None	2
11, 12, 13	Jive chassé L, R, L, on spot leading lady forward, on left side	None	3 a 4

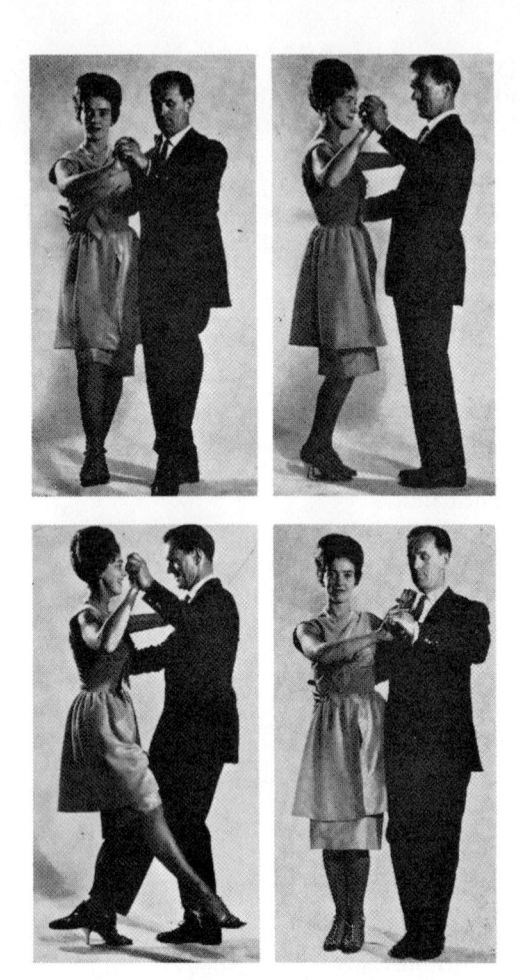

JIVE—KICKING THROUGH VARIATION
Steps 3, 4
Steps 7, 8

JIVE—KICKING THROUGH VARIATION
Steps 5, 6
Steps 9, 10

Step	Feet Positions	Amount of Turn	Timing
14, 15, 16	Jive chassé R, L, R, on spot and turning lady to her right, releasing her with left hand	None	3 a 4

Footwork. Ball of foot or ball flat on each step.

Lady. Commences with right hand in gentleman's right hand

1	RF back	None	1
2	Replace weight on LF	None	2
3, 4, 5	Jive chassé R, L, R, turning under partner's raised right arm	$\frac{1}{2}$ turn to left	3 a 4
6, 7, 8	Jive chassé L, R, L, moving slightly to left	None	3 a 4
9	RF back	None	1
10	Replace weight on LF	None	2
11, 12, 13	Jive chassé R, L, R, moving forwards	Commence to turn to right	3 a 4
14, 15, 16	Jive chassé L, R, L	Continue to turn to R completing $1\frac{1}{2}$ turns to R	3 a 4

Footwork. Ball of foot or ball flat on each step.

Exit. Change of Places Left to Right.

EXAMINATION QUESTIONS AND ANSWERS
Jive for Associates

Basic Movement

Q. Is this figure used often by experienced Jive dancers?

A. No, it is a good exercise for beginners to help master the rhythm. When they become good dancers they substitute the Whip which has the same timing and uses the same footwork.

Q. Are any other figures used mainly as an exercise?
A. Yes, the Basic Fallaway, and Basic Throwaway.

Link

Q. Why was this step named the Link?
A. This step was so named because it links the couple from an open to a closed position.

Change of Places Right to Left

Q. How does the gentleman lead the lady into this movement?
A. On the first 1, 2, 3 a 4 he leads her mainly with his right hand, on the second 3 a 4 he raises his left hand and leads her with his right and his left hand to turn right.

Change of Places Left to Right

Q. How does the gentleman lead the lady into this movement?
A. The lady cannot be led on the count of 1 because the couple are only holding with his left and her right hand, therefore she must know that she has to step back on her RF for 1; then the gentleman leads with his left hand to bring her forward on 2, also to turn her to the left on the first 3 a 4 and then follow her as she travels back LRL on the second 3 a 4.

The Whip

Q. How much turn is usually made as gentleman?

A. Five-eighths turn to the right, but more can be made.

Q. On which steps would the extra turn be made?

A. Usually on the first two steps 1, 2, R. L.

Q. Would this apply to the Throwaway Whip?

A. Yes.

American Spin

Q. Should the lady close her RF to her LF on the first step?

A. No, she must step back.

Members' and Fellows' Syllabus

Simple Spin

Q. Why was this step named the Simple Spin when it is more difficult than the American Spin?

A. Because there are only two steps and the American Spin has 4 steps.

Stop and Go

Q. How does the gentleman lead this movement?

A. Having led the lady into the 1, 2, 3 a 4 of the Change of Places Left to Right he braces his left arm on the count of 1 and he places his right hand on her back. On count 2 he leads her forward with his right hand and she then completes the second 3 a 4 of Change of Places Right to Left.

Spanish Arms

Q. How much turn does the lady make?

A. She makes a quarter turn to the left on the first

3 a 4 and five-eighths of a turn to the right on the second 3 a 4.

Q. Can she make more turn?

A. Yes, she can make three-eighths of a turn to the left on the first 3 a 4, and three-quarters of a turn to right on the second 3 a 4.

Windmill

Q. Is there a strong lean on this step?

A. No, the gentleman gets a slight lean to left on the first 3 a 4 and slight lean to the right on the second 3 a 4. The lady normal opposite.

Rolling off the Arm

Q. What is the entry for this figure?

A. Basically the Change of Places Right to Left with change of hands, therefore the gentleman has the lady's right hand in his right hand. The Rolling off the Arm is also used as a finish to the Windmill, in this case the lady's left hand is in the gentleman's right hand.

Chicken Walks

Q. Does the lady advance forward on the heels or toes?

A. Definitely on the heels, she leans well back and her partner braces his left arm and leads her forward, but the steps must be very short.

SECTION V

THE CHA CHA CHA

This dance we learned in the ballrooms of Cuba. There the dancers did not at first intend it to be a new dance, they were aware that extra beats were appearing in the Rumba music, and as the Cubans are probably the most rhythmic dancers in the world it was perfectly natural for them to mark these beats with their feet. So the Cha Cha Cha was born. On our return, we introduced this dance but it was not until some years later when our bands began to play Cha Cha Chas, that it became generally known.

All the following steps were learned by Pierre and myself in Cuba, either from Pepe Rivera or from our visits to the academias in Havana which, during our stay we visited *every* evening from 10 p.m. till 4 a.m.

Pierre and I named all the steps—as we did for all the other dances in this book—upon our return.

CHA CHA CHA

Tempo. 32–34 bars per minute.

Musical Timing. 4/4, 4 beats to each bar of music.

The first step is taken on the 2nd beat of the bar of music, counted 2 or S.

The second step is taken on the 3rd beat of the bar of music, counted 3 or S.

The 3rd and 4th steps are taken on the 4th beat of the bar of music, counted 4–and or QQ.

THE CHA CHA CHA

The 5th step is taken on the 1st beat of the bar of music, counted 1 or S.

Note. If it is difficult to start on the second beat, try making a preliminary step on the first beat of the bar of music. When dancing to properly orchestrated music it is very easy to hear the Cha Cha Cha or 4 and one. The Cubans count "Step, Step, Cha Cha Cha."

Basic Movement

Entries. Alemana, Hockey Stick, Time Step, Spot Turn

Step	Feet Positions	Amount of Turn	Timing
Gentleman			
1	LF forward leaving RF in place	Commence to turn to left	2 or S
2	Replace weight on RF	Continue to turn to left	3 or S
3	LF to side	Approximately	4 or Q
4	Draw RF towards LF	$\frac{1}{8}$ turn to left between steps	"and" or Q
5	LF to side	1 and 5	1 or S
6	RF back, leaving LF in place	Commence to turn to left	2 or S
7	Replace weight on LF	Continue to turn to left	3 or S
8	RF to side	Approximately	4 or Q
9	Draw LF towards RF	$\frac{1}{8}$ turn to left between steps	"and" or Q
10	RF to side	6 and 10	1 or S

Lady

Normal opposite.

Footwork. Ball flat on each step.

Exits. Fan, New York, Shoulder to Shoulder, Cross Basic, Time Step, Natural Top after dancing steps 1–5.

146   LATIN AND AMERICAN DANCES

CHA CHA CHA—BASIC MOVEMENTS
Steps 1–3
Steps 4 and 5

Fan

Entry. Forward Half, Basic Movement, Cross Basic.

Step   Feet Positions   Amount of Turn   Timing

Gentleman

Dances steps 6–10 of the basic movement without turning, releasing lady with right hand on step 7.

Lady

6	LF forward	None	2 or S

THE CHA CHA CHA

7	RF back and slightly to side	¼ turn to left between steps	3 or S
8	LF back	7 and 10	4 or Q
9	Draw RF towards LF	—	"and" or Q
10	LF back	—	1 or S

Footwork. Ball flat on each step.

Exits. Alemana, Hockey Stick.

The Alemana

Entries. Fan, Hip Twist, or any Opening Out movement to gentleman's left side.

Step	Feet Positions	Amount of Turn	Timing
Gentleman			
1	LF forward leaving RF in place	None	2 or S
2	Replace weight on RF	None	3 or S
3	LF to side	None	4 or Q
4	Draw RF towards LF	None	"and" or Q
5	LF to side	None	1 or S
6	RF back, leaving LF in place	None	2 or S
7	Replace weight on LF	None	3 or S
8	RF to side	None	4 or Q
9	Draw LF towards RF	None	"and" or Q
10	RF to side	None	1 or S
Lady			
1	RF closes to LF	None	2 or S
2	LF forward	None	3 or S
3	RF forward	Commence to turn to right	4 or Q
4	Draw LF towards RF	one and a	"and" or Q

Step	Feet Positions	Amount of Turn	Timing
5	RF forward	quarter turns to	1 or S
6	LF forward	right between	2 or S
7	RF forward	steps 3 to 10	3 or S
8	LF forward	—	4 or Q
9	Draw RF towards LF	—	"and" or Q
10	LF forward	—	1 or S

Footwork. Ball flat on each step.

Note. As in the Rumba the lady can turn one and a half or one and three-quarter turns to right and follow with Closed Hip Twist or Spiral.

Exits. Basic Movement, Hand to Hand, Time Step, Cross Basic.

Hand to Hand

Entry. Alemana; releasing lady's right hand and taking her left hand in his right hand on step 8.

Step	Feet Positions	Amount of Turn	Timing
Gentleman			
1	LF back leaving RF in place	¼ turn to left	2 or S
2	Replace weight on RF	¼ turn to right between steps	3 or S
3	LF to side	2 and 3	4 or Q
4	Draw RF towards LF	None	"and" or Q
5	LF to side	None	1 or S
6	RF back, leaving LF in place	¼ turn to right	2 or S
7	Replace weight on LF	¼ turn to left between steps 7	3 or S
8	RF to side	and 8	4 or Q
9	Draw LF towards RF	None	"and" or Q
10	RF to side	None	1 or S

The above ten steps can be repeated *ad lib.*

THE CHA CHA CHA

CHA CHA CHA—HAND TO HAND
Steps 1–3
Steps 4–6

Footwork. Ball flat on each step.

Lady

Same steps as gentleman but commencing on RF and turning to right when he turns left and vice versa.

Note. On step 1 gentleman holds lady's left hand in his right hand and changes hands on step 3.

Exit. Basic movement.

The Hockey Stick

Entries. Fan, Hip Twist, any Opening Out to gentleman's left side.

Step	Feet Positions	Amount of Turn	Timing
Gentleman			
1	LF forward leaving RF in place	None	2 or S
2	Replace weight on RF	None	3 or S
3	LF to side	None	4 or Q
4	Draw RF towards LF	None	"and" or Q
5	LF to side	None	1 or S
6	RF back leaving LF in place	Commence to turn to right	2 or S
7	Replace weight on LF	$\frac{1}{8}$ turn to right between steps	3 or S
8	RF forward	6 and 10	4 or Q
9	Draw LF towards RF	—	"and" or Q
10	RF forward	—	1 or S
Lady			
1	RF closes to LF	None	2 or S
2	LF forward	None	3 or S
3	RF forward	None	4 or Q
4	Draw LF towards RF	None	"and" or Q
5	RF forward	—	1 or S
6	LF forward	Commence to turn to left	2 or S
7	RF back and slightly to side	$\frac{5}{8}$ turn to left between steps	3 or S
8	LF back	6 and 10	4 or Q
9	Draw RF towards LF	—	"and" or Q
10	LF back	—	1 or S

Footwork. Ball flat on each step.

Exits. Basic Movement, Time Step, Open Hip Twist, Spot Turn, Cross Basic.

THE CHA CHA CHA

Time Step

Entries. Basic Movement, Alemana, Hockey Stick.

Step	Feet Positions	Amount of Turn	Timing
Gentleman			
1	RF crosses behind LF, leaving LF in place	None	2 or S
2	Replace weight on LF	None	3 or S
3	RF to side	None	4 or Q
4	Draw LF towards RF	None	"and" or Q
5	RF to side	None	1 or S

Repeat same five steps as above commencing with LF.
Footwork. Ball flat on each step.

Note. Time step can be danced in a closed position or the gentleman can release his partner at the end of the Alemana or Hockey Stick and they would then dance it apart.

Lady
Same steps as gentleman but lady on LF when the gentleman is on RF.

Exits. Basic Movement, Cross Basic, Spot Turn.

Spot Turn

Usually danced apart.
Entry. Time Step.

Step	Feet Positions	Amount of Turn	Timing
Gentleman			
1	LF forward	A complete turn	2 or S
2	RF forward	is made to the	3 or S
3	LF to side	right between	4 or Q
4	Draw RF towards LF	steps 1 and 5 —	"and" or Q
5	LF to side		1 or S

Footwork. Ball flat on each step.

CHA CHA CHA—SPOT TURN
Steps 1–3
Steps 4 and 5

Lady

Same steps as gentleman and may be danced individually or at the same time with partners facing each other.

Note. Spot Turns can be danced turning to right or left.

Exits. Time Step, Basic Movement, Cross Basic.

THE CHA CHA CHA

Natural Top

Entries. Forward Basic Movement.

Step	Feet Positions	Amount of Turn	Timing
Gentleman			
1	RF placed behind LF	Turning to right	2 or S
2	LF to side and slightly forward	The amount of turn in the 15 steps can vary with the speed of the music or the ability of the dancers, etc., up to two complete turns can be made	3 or S
3	RF moves towards LF		4 or Q
4	LF to side		"and" or Q
5	RF moves towards LF		1 or S
6	LF to side and slightly forward		2 or S
7	RF crosses behind LF		3 or S
8	LF to side		4 or Q
9	RF moves towards LF		"and" or Q
10	LF to side		1 or S

Repeat steps 1, 2, 3, 4, 5.

Footwork. Ball or ball flat on steps 1 and 7, ball flat on the remaining steps.

Lady			
1	LF to side and slightly back		2 or S
2	RF placed in front of LF	Same as the gentleman	3 or S
3	LF to side and slightly back		4 or Q
4	RF placed in front of LF		"and" or Q
5	LF to side and slightly back		1 or S
6	RF placed in front of LF		2 or S

Step	Feet Positions	Amount of Turn	Timing
7	LF to side and slightly back		3 or S
8	RF placed in front of LF		4 or Q
9	LF to side and slightly back		"and" or Q
10	RF placed in front of LF		1 or S

Repeat steps 1, 2, 3, 4, 5.

Footwork. Ball flat on each step.

Exits. Opening Out as from Natural Top.

Opening Out as from Natural Top

Entry. Natural Top.

Step	Feet Positions	Amount of Turn	Timing
Gentleman			
1	LF to side or forward, leaving RF in place	None	2 or S
2	Replace weight on RF	None	3 or S
3	LF to side	None	4 or Q
4	Draw RF towards LF	None	"and" or Q
5	LF to side	None	1 or S
Lady			
1	RF back and slightly to side	Approximately $\frac{1}{2}$ turn to right	2 or S
2	Replace weight on LF	Approximately $\frac{1}{2}$ turn to left between steps 2, 3	3 or S
3	RF to side		4 or Q

THE CHA CHA CHA 155

| 4 | Draw LF towards RF | None | "and" or Q |
| 5 | RF to side | None | 1 or S |

Footwork. Ball flat on each step.

Exits. Closed Hip Twist, Spiral, Steps 6–10 of **Basic** Movement.

Closed Hip Twist

Entry. Opening out as from Natural Top.

Step	Feet Positions	Amount of Turn	Timing
Gentleman			
1	RF back leaving LF in place releasing lady with R hand	None	2 or S
2	Replace weight on LF	None	3 or S
3	RF to side	None	4 or Q
4	Draw LF towards RF	None	"and" or Q
5	RF to side	None	1 or S
Lady			
1	LF forward	$\frac{3}{8}$ turn to right	2 or S
2	RF back and slightly to side	$\frac{5}{8}$ turn to left between steps 2, 5	3 or S
3	LF back		4 or Q
4	Draw RF towards LF	—	"and" or Q
5	LF back	—	1 or S

Footwork. Ball flat on each step.

Exits. Alemana, Hockey Stick.

Cross Basic

Entries. Basic Movement, Alemana, Hockey Stick, Time Step.

Step	Feet Positions	Amount of Turn	Timing
Gentleman			
1	LF crosses in front of RF	Approximately ¼ turn to left between steps 1 and 5	2 or S
2	RF back		3 or S
3	LF to side		4 or Q
4	Draw RF towards LF	—	"and" or Q
5	LF to side	—	1 or S
6	RF crosses behind LF	Approximately ¼ turn to left between steps 6 and 10	2 or S
7	LF forward		3 or S
8	RF to side		4 or Q
9	Draw LF towards RF	—	"and" or Q
10	RF to side	—	1 or S

Lady
Normal opposite.

Footwork. Ball flat on each step.

Exits. Basic Movement, Fan.

Shoulder to Shoulder

Entry. Basic Movement (first five steps).

Step	Feet Positions	Amount of Turn	Timing
Gentleman			
1	RF back, leaving LF in place	⅛ to R	2 or S
2	Replace weight forward on LF	⅛ turn to left between steps 2 and 5	3 or S
3	RF to side		4 or Q
4	Draw LF towards RF	—	"and" or Q
5	RF to side	—	1 or S

THE CHA CHA CHA

6	LF back, leaving RF in place	⅛ turn to left	2 or S
7	Replace weight forward on RF	⅛ turn to right between steps	3 or S
8	LF to side	7 and 10	4 or Q
9	Draw RF towards LF	—	"and" or Q
10	LF to side	—	1 or S

Footwork. Ball flat on each step.

Lady

1	LF forward outside partner on left side leaving RF in place	⅛ turn to right	2 or S
2	Replace weight on RF	⅛ turn to left between steps	3 or S
3	LF to side	2 and 5	4 or Q
4	Draw RF towards LF	—	"and" or Q
5	LF to side	—	1 or S
6	RF forward outside partner on right side leaving LF in place	⅛ turn to left	2 or S
7	Replace weight on LF	⅛ turn to right between steps	3 or S
8	RF to side	7 and 10	4 or Q
9	Draw LF towards RF	—	"and" or Q
10	RF to side		1 or S

Footwork. Ball flat on each step.

Exit. Backward Basic Movement, Spot Turns.

Note. The Shoulder to Shoulder can also be preceded by the Hockey Stick. The gentleman would then dance the lady's steps 1 to 10 and the lady would dance the gentleman's steps 1 to 10 as described above. This movement can be danced with or without hold.

The New York Step

Entry. Basic Movement, releasing hold of lady with right hand.

Step	Feet Positions	Amount of Turn	Timing
Gentleman			
1	LF forward leaving RF in place	¼ turn to right	2 or S
2	Replace weight on RF	¼ turn to left between steps 2 and 3	3 or S
3	LF to side		4 or Q
4	Draw RF towards LF	None	"and" or Q
5	LF to side releasing lady's hand and taking her L hand in his R hand	None	1 or S
6	RF forward leaving LF in place	¼ turn to left	2 or S
7	Replace weight on LF	¼ turn to right between steps 7 and 8	3 or S
8	RF to side		4 or Q
9	Draw LF towards RF	None	"and" or Q
10	RF to side	None	1 or S

The above ten steps can be repeated *ad lib.*

Lady

Same steps as gentleman but lady commences with RF and turning to left when he turns right and vice versa.

Footwork. Ball flat on each step.

Exits. Basic Movement, Spot Turn.

Open Hip Twist

Entries. Fan, Closed Hip Twist, Open Hip Twist, Hockey Stick, Spiral.

THE CHA CHA CHA

Step	Feet Positions	Amount of Turn	Timing
Gentleman			
1	LF forward leaving RF in place	None	2 or S
2	Replace weight on RF	None	3 or S
3	LF to side	None	4 or Q
4	Draw RF towards LF	None	"and" or Q
5	LF to side	None	1 or S
6	RF back leaving LF in place	$\frac{1}{4}$ turn to left between steps	2 or S
7	Replace weight on LF	6 and 10	3 or S
8	RF to side, small step	—	4 or Q
9	Draw LF towards RF	—	"and" or Q
10	RF to side, small step	—	1 or S
Lady			
1	RF closes to LF	None	2 or S
2	LF forward	None	3 or S
3	RF forward	None	4 or Q
4	Draw LF towards RF	None	"and" or Q
5	RF forward	None	1 or S
6	LF forward	$\frac{3}{8}$ turn to right	2 or S
7	RF back and slightly to side	$\frac{5}{8}$ turn to left between steps	3 or S
8	LF back	7 and 10	4 or Q
9	Draw RF towards LF	—	"and" or Q
10	LF back	—	1 or S

Footwork. Ball flat on each step.

Exits. Open Hip Twist, Natural Top after first five steps of above figure or Hockey Stick, or Alemana if gentleman does not turn on steps 6 to 10.

160   LATIN AND AMERICAN DANCES

The Spiral

Entry. Opening out as from Natural Top.

Step	Feet Positions	Amount of Turn	Timing
Gentleman			
1	LF to side releasing lady with R hand	None	1 or S
2	RF back leaving LF in place	None	2 or S
3	Replace weight on LF		3 or S
4	RF to side and slightly forward	Approximately ⅛ turn to left	4 or Q
5	Draw LF towards RF	between steps 3 and 6	"and" or Q
6	RF to side and slightly forward		1 or S
Lady			
1	RF to side facing partner at commencement of step turn on RF with knees locked	½ turn to left	1 or S
2	LF forward	⅛ turn to left	2 or S
3	RF back and slightly to side	Approximately ½ turn to left	3 or S
4	LF back	between steps 3 and 6	4 or Q
5	Draw RF towards LF		"and" or Q
6	LF back	—	1 or S

Footwork. Ball flat on each step.

Exits. Open Hip Twist, Time Step, Spot Turn.

Amalgamation

Gentleman

Commence backing diagonally to centre.

THE CHA CHA CHA

Basic Movement, forward half, finish facing wall.
Fan, facing wall.
Alemana, facing wall, releasing lady's right hand.
Time Step, commence LF.
Time Step, commence RF.
Spot Turn to right, finish facing wall.
Time Step, commence RF facing wall.
Basic Movement, forward half, no turn (lady now in normal hold).
Fan, facing wall.
Overturned Alemana, finish facing wall with lady's left hand in gentleman's right hand having released hold with left hand.
Hand to Hand, four times, finish facing wall.
Basic Movement, facing wall, no turn.
Fan, facing wall.
Hockey Stick, finish backing diagonally to centre.
Repeat from beginning.

Lady

Commence facing diagonally to centre.
Basic Movement, backward half, finish backing wall.
Fan, finish backing L.O.D.
Alemana, finish backing wall.
Time Step, commence RF.
Time Step, commence LF.
Time Step, commence RF.
Spot Turn to right, finish backing wall.
Basic Movement, backward half, backing wall no turn.
Fan, finish backing L.O.D.
Overturned Alemana, finish facing L.O.D.
Hand to Hand, four times, finish backing wall.
Basic Movement, backing wall, no turn.
Fan, finish backing L.O.D.
Hockey Stick, finish facing diagonally to centre.
Repeat from beginning.

Reverse Top

The steps are similar to the Rumba Reverse Top, described on page 14, but there is no pause on count 4, a Cha Cha Cha chassé is danced to the count of 4 and 1, therefore if a full Top is danced there are fifteen counts instead of nine.

Opening Out from Reverse Top

Here again similar steps are danced, as described on pages 17–18, again no pause on 4 but carried on for a Cha Cha Cha chassé, count 4 and 1, therefore the Opening Out would take five counts.

Aida

This figure can be preceded by the Hand to Hand or 10 Steps of a Reverse Top and again using the Cha Cha Cha chassé.

The *Aida* which is now only 3 steps, described on page 168, would take 5 counts.

The Advanced Hip Twist as described on page 31 and usually preceded by stepping forward on the 9th count of a Natural Top would, when danced in the Cha Cha Cha, after each count of 4, *and* 1, be added, making 10 steps instead of 6.

The Heel Toe Variation (*see page* 164)

This step is danced in solo position, the lady and gentleman standing about two feet apart and not holding. The arms and shoulders should be relaxed. It is from the waist downwards that the movement is expressed. This movement can be preceded by the Alemana or Hockey Stick, the gentleman releasing hold with both hands at the end of the movement when he is on his right foot and the lady on her left foot. Continue as follows—

Step	Feet Positions	Amount of Turn	Timing
Gentleman			
1	LF to side, toe turned out, with part weight	None	2 or S
2	Place left toe to right instep, part weight	None	3 or S
3	LF to side	None	4 or Q
4	Draw RF slightly towards LF	None	"and" or Q
5	LF to side	None	1 or S

Lady

Dances the same steps, but when the gentleman is on his right foot she is on her left foot and vice versa.

Footwork. Heel on step 1, toe on step 2, ball flat on steps 3, 4, 5.

Exits. Basic Movement or Cross Basic.

EXAMINATION QUESTIONS AND ANSWERS

Cha Cha Cha for Associates

Q. Are the Cha Cha Cha beats even?
A. Yes, ½ beat, ½ beat, and 1 beat.

Hand to Hand

Q. On the Cha Cha Cha should the couple be back to back?
A. No, the gentleman's right shoulder is either level with her left shoulder or his left shoulder level with her right.

Time Step

Q. Is there any turn?
A. No, the movement is danced facing each other.

CHA CHA CHA—HEEL TOE VARIATION
Steps 1, 2
Steps 3 and 5; Step 4

Spot Turn

Q. Should this be turned to right or left?

A. Both, but when turned right it is usual to start with the LF and vice versa.

Natural Top

Q. Should the gentleman cross on the Cha Cha Chas?

A. No, a normal Cha Cha Cha chassé is danced but continuing to turn slightly rightwards.

Opening Out from Natural Top

Q. Does the gentleman step to the side on step 1?

A. He can but it is more natural to step forward.

Cross Basic

Q. Are the steps the same length as in the basic movement?

A. They are just a little longer, that is on the second and seventh steps.

Shoulder to Shoulder

Q. Does the gentleman always step back and the lady forward on the first step?

A. No the lady can step back and the gentleman forward. If taken from the forward half of basic movement, the gentleman would step back on the first step, but if danced after a Hockey Stick the gentleman could step forward on step 1, the lady normal opposite.

Open Hip Twist

Q. Does the lady turn on the first Cha Cha Cha?

A. No, she dances the Cha Cha Cha forward and turns on the next step.

Spiral

Q. Is the amount of turn the same as the Spiral in the Rumba?

A. Basically yes, but as in the Rumba more turn can be made.

SECTION VI

STANDARDIZED VARIATIONS

The movements described in this section are variations of the main Latin American dances which have stood the test of time. Monsieur Pierre and I learnt almost all of them during our various visits to Cuba, Brazil and America, and we gave them names on our return to Britain. The movements have been introduced by Dancing Societies at their Congresses and have since been officially taught all over the British Isles and in many European countries, as also in America, Australia, Canada, Japan, New Zealand, etc.

The Imperial Society of Teachers of Dancing Incorporated have now decided to increase the number of figures on their syllabus for Latin American dances and have selected the movements contained in this section.

RUMBA

Alternative Basic

Described on page 5.

Hand to Hand

This movement is similar to the Hand to Hand as described on page 148, but dance steps 4, 5 and 9, 10 are omitted. The timing would thus be counted 4–1 or S on step 3, and 4–1 or slow on step 8.

Aida

Entry. 6 steps of the Reverse Top.

Step	Feet Positions	Amount of Turn	Timing
Gentleman			
1	RF back releasing lady with R hand	Curving to R	2 or Q
2	LF back	Still turning to R	3 or Q
3	RF back	Still turning completing approx. $\frac{3}{8}$ turn to R	4–1 or S
4	LF forward	Commence to turn L	2 or Q
5	RF forward	Continue to turn L	3 or Q
6	LF forward	Continue to turn L to finish facing partner having turned 1$\frac{3}{8}$ turns to L	4–1 or S
7, 8, 9	Repeat steps 4, 5, 6 but RF, LF, RF	Making 1 full turn to L to again finish facing partner	2, 3, 4–1 or Q Q S

Lady

The lady dances the same steps as the gentleman but when he is on his LF she is on RF and vice versa and when he turns to R she turns to L and when he to L she turns to R.

Footwork. Ball flat on each step.

Exits. Basic Movement or Progressive Walk.

Note. It is also correct for the lady and gentleman on steps 4, 5, 6 to rock forward, rock back, rock forward and then both dance the spot turn, finishing facing partner. On step 6 both lady and gentleman commence to turn—gentleman to L and lady to R.

Fencing

Entry. Commence in Fan position.

Step	Feet Positions	Amount of Turn	Timing
Gentleman			
1	LF forward	None	2 or Q
2	Replace weight on RF	None	3 or Q
3	LF to side	None	4–1 or S
4	RF forward with L arm and lady's R arm outstretched and sharply turning	¼ to L	2 or Q
5	Replace weight on LF	Commencing to turn to R	3 or Q
6	RF to side completing ¼ turn to R, immediately turning a full turn to R with pressure on ball of RF	1¼ to R	4–1 or S

Exit. Basic Movement or backward progressive walk.

Lady			
1	RF closes to LF	None	2 or Q
2	LF forward	None	3 or Q
3	RF forward	Commencing to turn to R	4–1 or S
4	LF forward turning sharply to R	½ turn to R	2 or Q
5	Replace weight on RF	Commencing to turn to L	3 or Q
6	LF to side completing ¼ turn to L immediately turning a full turn to L with pressure on ball of LF	1¼ to L	4–1 or S

Note. On step 6 having stepped to the side both lady and gentleman can dance a Spot Turn, he to the right, L, R, L, and she to the left, R, L, R,

    2 3 4–1
    or
    Q Q S

Footwork. Ball flat on each step, except step 6.
Exit. Basic Movement, Progressive Walk.

Kiki Walks

Entry. Overturned Alemana, lady turning $1\frac{3}{4}$ turns to R finishing on Gentleman's R side and facing the same way as he.

Step	Feet Positions	Amount of Turn	Timing
Gentleman			
1	LF back	None	2 or Q
2	RF forward	None	3 or Q
3	LF forward	Curving slightly to L	4–1 or S
4	RF forward	Curving slightly to L	2 or Q
5	LF forward	Curving slightly to L	3 or Q
6	RF forward	Curving slightly to L	4–1 or S
7	LF forward	Curving slightly to L	2 or Q
8	RF forward	Curving slightly to L	3 or Q
9	LF to side	Turning $\frac{1}{4}$ turn to R	4–1 or S
Lady			
1	RF back	None	2 or Q
2	LF forward	None	3 or Q
3	RF forward	Curving slightly to L	4–1 or S
4	LF forward	Curving slightly to L	2 or Q

STANDARDIZED VARIATIONS

Step	Feet Positions	Amount of Turn	Timing
5	RF forward	Curving slightly to L	3 or Q
6	LF forward	Curving slightly to L	4–1 or S
7	RF forward	Curving slightly to L	2 or Q
8	LF forward	Curving slightly to L	3 or Q
9	RF to side	Turning ¼ turn to L	4–1 or S

Footwork. Ball flat on each step.

Exits. Second half of Basic Movement, or continue curving on step 9 and dance The Spiral or Open Lady out into Fan position.

Movement of the Hips in the Rumba

The body from the waist upwards should be kept quite motionless but relaxed. When one of the legs is braced the hips should swing to the side of the leg in question. However, this does not happen immediately the weight is transferred from one leg to the other, as the bracing must be done gradually.

A simple description of the hips' movement is as follows: commence with the feet together and the weight on the right foot; the right knee should be braced and the left knee bent. Transfer weight on to the left foot, at the same time straightening the knee and swinging the hips slowly to the left to the count of 2. The left knee should now be braced and the right knee bent. Transfer weight on to the right foot, at the same time straightening the knee while the hips slowly swing to the right to the count of 3. The right knee should now be braced and the left knee bent. Transfer weight on to the left foot, straightening the left knee, while the hips slowly swing to the left to the count of

4–1. The left knee should now be braced and the right knee bent.

Note. On the count of 4 the hips begin to swing to the left and on the count of 1 the left hip is out to its fullest extent.

When this exercise has been mastered the same system can be applied to the Basic Movements, Progressive Walk, Fan and Hockey stick.

SAMBA
Rolling off the Arm

This movement is usually danced facing L.O.D.

Entry. The Shadow Bota Fogo having turned lady $1\frac{1}{8}$ turns to right and to finish in PP holding her L hand in his R hand across her body, followed by Samba Walk R, L, R.

Step	Feet Positions	Amount of Turn	Timing
Gentleman			
1, 2, 3	A flat whisk to side L, R, L leading lady to turn to her R	None	1 a 2
4, 5, 6	A flat whisk to side R, L, R leading lady to turn to her L	None	1 a 2
7, 8, 9	Repeat steps 1, 2, 3	None	1 a 2
10, 11, 12	A flat whisk to side R, L, R facing partner	$\frac{1}{4}$ to R	1 a 2
Lady			
	Preceded by Samba Walk L, R, L		1 a 2
1	RF forward	Commencing to turn approx. $\frac{1}{4}$ to R	1
2	LF to side	Still turning to R approx. $\frac{1}{4}$	a

Step	Feet Positions	Amount of Turn	Timing
3	RF to side	Completing a full turn to R	2
4	LF forward	Approx. ¼ turn commencing to turn L	1
5	RF to side	Approx. ¼ turn still turning to L	a
6	LF to side	Completing a full turn to L	2
7, 8, 9	Repeat steps 1, 2, 3		1 a 2
10, 11, 12	Repeat steps 4, 5, 6	Turning 1¼ turns to L to finish facing partner	1 a 2

On the last step gentleman releases lady's L hand. He regains normal hold and follows with a whisk to left. This movement can also be danced dancing two Samba walks in PP between steps 6, 7, gentleman L, R, L, R, L, R. lady R, L, R, L, R, L, count 1 a 2, 1 a 2.

Footwork. Gentleman the same as in dancing the Whisk. Lady heel flat on steps 1 and 4, ball flat on steps 2, 3, 5 and 6.

Exit. Whisk to L.

Changes of Feet

Entry. The Natural Basic Movement R, L, R, L, R, L, count 1 a 2, 1 a 2 then:—This movement is usually commenced facing L.O.D.

Step	Feet Positions	Amount of Turn	Timing
Gentleman			
1	RF forward leading lady with his R hand to turn to L	None	1
2	Short step forward with LF	None	2

Step	Feet Positions	Amount of Turn	Timing
Lady			
1	LF back	Commencing to turn to L	1
2	RF closes to LF	Still turning to L	a
3	Replace weight on LF	Having turned ½ turn to L	2

Lady is now in man's R arm and facing the same way as he.

Both lady and gentleman now have their weight on the LF.

Footwork. Ball flat on each step.

They could continue with four Bota Fogo's (travelling) R, L, R, L, R, L, R, L, R, L, R, L, counting 1 a 2, 1 a 2, 1 a 2, 1 a 2.	None	

Exits. Follow with another Change of Feet. Two possibilities are as follows:

I *Gentleman*

1	RF forward	None	1
2	LF closes to RF (with weight on LF)	None	2

Lady

1	RF forward	Commencing to turn to R	1
2	Close LF to RF	Still turning to R	a
3	Replace weight on RF	Having turned ½ turn to R	2

Footwork. Ball flat on each step.

Exits. Basic Movement Natural Roll.

II The lady turns ½ turn to her left on the 4th Bota Fogo to finish in Cum Batu position. Follow with the contra Bota Fogo and dance the Cum Batu.

Exit. Bota Fogos in the PP and CPP.

Note. The Cum Batu is described on page 67.

The Volta

This movement is described on pages 65–66.

The Volta can be danced with practically no turn and can also be turned to the right.

A slight dropping action can be used.

Shadow Bota Fogo

Entry. Side Samba Walk, leading lady slightly forward.

Step	Feet Positions	Amount of Turn	Timing
Gentleman			
1–3	Travelling Bota Fogo on L, R, L, raising L arm leading lady into Bota Fogo in front; assist this lead with R hand, then release. Lady now in front of gentleman on his L side	¼ to L	1 a 2
4–6	Travelling Bota Fogo on R, L, R, keeping L arm high leading Lady into Bota Fogo in front	¼ to R	1 a 2
7–9	Repeat steps 1–3, leading lady leftwards with left hand only	¼ to L	1 a 2

Step	Feet Positions	Amount of Turn	Timing
10–12	Repeat steps 4–6, leading lady rightwards with left hand only	¼ to R	1 a 2

Exit. Small forward Samba Walk on L, R, L, turning lady under L arm to her R (1 a 2) into Natural basic; Progressive basic; or (if overturned to PP), Samba Walk.

Lady

Step	Feet Positions	Amount of Turn	Timing
1–3	Travelling Bota Fogo on R, L, R, passing across in front of gentleman, keeping R arm high	¼ to R	1 a 2
4–6	Travelling Bota Fogo on L, R, L, passing across in front of gentleman keeping R arm high	¼ to L	1 a 2
7–9	Repeat steps 1–3	¼ to R	1 a 2
10–12	Repeat steps 4–6	¼ to L	1 a 2
13	Step on RF	Turning to R	1
14	Close LF towards RF	Still turning to R	a
15	Step in place on RF	Still turning to R approx. ¾ turn R to face partner, or 1⅛ turn R to finish in PP	2

Footwork. As in travelling Bota Fogo.

Exit. Basic Movement Natural Roll or Rolling off the Arm.

The Criss Cross or Travelling Volta

In Basic Form Commence facing L.O.D.

Entry. Side Samba Walk, moving slightly forward in front of Lady.

STANDARDIZED VARIATIONS

Step	Feet Positions	Amount of Turn	Timing
Gentleman			
1	Cross LF slightly in front of RF	None	1
2	Side and slightly back RF small step	None	a
3–6	Repeat steps 1–2 twice Raising L arm, release hold with R hand and lead lady to pass gradually behind Gentleman's back	None	2 a 3 a
7	Cross LF slightly in front of RF lady now on gentleman's L side	None	4
8	Cross RF slightly in front of LF	None	1
9	Side and slightly back LF	Curving gradually to R $\frac{1}{4}$ turn to finish facing wall	a
10–13	Repeat steps 8–9 twice keeping L arm high; lead lady to pass in front		2 a 3 a
14	Cross RF slightly in front of LF resume normal hold at end.		4
Lady			
1	Cross RF slightly in front of LF	None	1

Step	Feet Positions	Amount of Turn	Timing
2	Side and slightly back LF small step	None	a
3–6	Repeat steps 1–2 twice, Raising right arm gradually passing behind gentleman's back	None	2 a 3 a
7	Cross RF slightly in front of LF now on Gentleman's L side	None	4
8	Cross LF slightly in front of RF	Curving gradually to L, ¼ turn, end facing him and backing wall	1
9	Side and slightly back RF		a
10–13	Repeat steps 8–9 twice	None	2 a 3 a
14	Cross LF slightly in front of RF		4

Note. After the first half of this movement (steps 1–7) it is permissible to dance Forward Samba Walk, followed by a Side Samba Walk (in which the gentleman dances the lady's steps and vice versa); this is danced facing L.O.D., with the lady on gentleman's L side. He leads the Side Samba Walk with pressure from his L hand. Continue with second half (steps 8–14) as before.

Footwork. Ball flat on steps 1, 3, 5, 7, 8, 10, 12 and 14. Ball of foot on steps 2, 4, 6, 9, 11 and 13.

Exit. Whisk to left.

STANDARDIZED VARIATIONS

Argentine Crosses

Entries. Side Samba Walk, turned $\frac{1}{4}$ to R lady turning $\frac{1}{4}$ to L to face partner; Stationary Samba Walk R, L, R.

Step	Feet Positions	Amount of Turn	Timing
Gentleman			
1	Forward LF outside partner on R side leading lady forward and leaning to L	Commence to circle to R	1
2	Cross RF lightly behind LF leaning to L	Continue to circle R	a
3	Forward LF still leaning to L	Continue to circle R	2
4	Forward RF leaning to R	Continue to circle R	1
5	Cross LF lightly behind RF leaning to R	Continue to circle R	a
6	Forward RF still leaning to R	Continue to circle R	2
7–12	Repeat steps 1–6, on L, R, L, R, L, R.		1 a 2
13–15	Small Forward Samba Walk on L, R, L, turning lady under L arm to her R (as described as exit to Shadow Bota Fogo).		1 a 2

Exits. Natural Basic, Progressive Basic, Corta Jaca (the latter two if gentleman makes turn to R on steps 13–15 to face diag. wall).

Step	Feet Positions	Amount of Turn	Timing
Lady			
1	Forward RF on partner's R side leaning to R	Commence to circle to R	1
2	Cross LF lightly behind RF leaning to R	Continue to circle to R	a
3	Forward RF still leaning to R	Continue to circle to R	2
4	Forward LF leaning to L	Continue to circle to R	1
5	Cross RF lightly behind LF leaning to L	Continue to circle to R	a
6	Forward LF leaning to L Still outside partner on his R side	Continue to circle to R	2
7–12	Repeat steps 1–6 on R, L, R, L, R, L		1 a 2
13–15	Turn under gentleman's L arm to R, RF, LF, RF, to end facing him.		1 a 2

Footwork. Ball flat on steps 1, 3, 4 and 6. Ball of foot on steps 2 and 5.

Exit. Basic Movement, Natural Roll. (The Natural Roll is described on pages 64–65.)

STANDARDIZED VARIATIONS

PASO DOBLE

Usually commenced facing L.O.D. on diag. to centre.

Left Foot Variation

Step	Feet Positions	Amount of Turn	Footwork	Timing
Gentleman				
1	LF forward	None	Heel flat	1
2	RF forward	None	Heel flat	2
3	LF forward preparing to step outside partner	None	Heel flat	1
4	Point RF forward (partner outside) without weight	None	Toe	2 (¾)
5	Close RF to LF	None	Ball flat	a (¼)
6	Point LF to side without weight	None	Toe	1
7	Close LF to RF	None	Ball flat	2
8	RF to side	None	Ball flat	1
9	Close LF to RF	None	Ball flat	2
Lady				
1	RF back	None	Ball flat	1
2	LF back	None	Ball flat	2
3	RF back	None	Ball flat	1
4	Point LF back (partner outside) without weight	None	Toe	2 (¾)
5	Close LF to RF	None	Ball flat	a (¼)
6	Point RF to side without weight	None	Toe	1
7	Close RF to LF	None	Ball flat	2
8	LF to side	None	Ball flat	1
9	Close RF to LF	None	Ball flat	2

Exit. Sur Place.

The Coup de Pique

Described on page 101.

The Fallaway Ending to Separation

Described on page 86.

Advanced Ending to Promenades

Described on page 91.

The Fregolina

Usually commenced facing wall.

Step	Feet Positions	Amount of Turn	Timing
Gentleman			
Entry. Dance the first thirteen steps of the "sixteen" extending the arms and taking the lady's L hand in R hand on step 13.			1, 2, 1, 2, 1, 2, 1, 2, 1, 1, 2, 1
	The gentleman's position is back to wall		
14	Mark time on LF (lady steps back RF), gentleman stands with feet together for the next 18 steps	None	2
1–4	Lead lady forward to pass from his R to L side, raising the R arm and lowering the L to turn her to the L under the raised arms on the 4th step	None	1, 2, 1, 2
5–8	While the lady takes 4 steps forward behind	None	1, 2, 1, 2

STANDARDIZED VARIATIONS

Step	Feet Positions	Amount of Turn	Timing
	gentleman's back, he has his L arm across his back at waist level and his R arm extended		
9–12	When she walks back for 4 steps the arms' position is reversed	None	1, 2, 1, 2
13–16	Repeat 5–8 leading lady around in front of gentleman on step 16, having released hold of her R hand on step 15	None	1, 2, 1, 2
17–18	Lead Lady to turn to her R with R hand and release hold. Take normal hold and dance	None	1, 2
19–22	Two side chassés RL, RL	None	1, 2, 1, 2

Footwork. Ball flat on steps 19, 20, 21 and 22.

Exit. Sur place.

Note. An alternative ending is for gentleman to turn up to a ¼ turn to R. on step 16, and so lessen the lady's turn to face him on this step.

Lady

Entry. Dance the first thirteen steps of the "Sixteen", then step back RF turning approx. ¼ turn to R, arms extended. The lady's position is on gentleman's R side facing against L.O.D.

1, 2, 1, 2,
1, 2, 1, 2,
1, 2, 1, 2,
1, 2

Step	Feet Positions	Amount of Turn	Footwork	Timing
1	LF forward	None	Heel flat	1
2	RF forward	None	Heel flat	2
3	LF forward (lady is now at gentleman's L side)	Commence to turn L	Heel flat	
4	RF forward (lady's R shoulder is in contact with gentleman's L shoulder during the turn to face wall)	Complete just over full turn to L	Ball, heel, ball	2
5	LF forward	None	Heel flat	1
6	RF forward	None	Heel flat	2
7	LF forward	Curving L	Heel flat	1
8	RF forward	Completing ½ to L	Heel flat	2

Note. During the last four steps lady has passed behind gentleman's back from his L to R side and both on step 8 are back to wall.

9	LF back	Curving R	Ball flat	1
10	RF back	None	Ball flat	2
11	LF back	None	Ball flat	1
12	RF back	Curving to R	Ball flat	2

Note. During the last four steps lady has passed behind gentleman's back from his R side to his L side.

13–16	Repeat steps 5–8 turning to finish in front of partner on step 16	Approx. ⅝ to L	Heel flat on steps 13–15; ball flat on 16	1, 2, 1, 2
17–18	Turn to R, LF, RF, to face square to partner	Full turn	Ball flat	1, 2
19–22	Dance two Side Chassés, L, R, L, R	None	Ball flat	1, 2, 1, 2

Exit. Sur Place.

The Farol

Both the lady and gentleman dance the same entry as the Fregolina. They then dance steps 1 to 8 but gentleman releases lady's right hand on step 7 and leads her to face him on step 8.

They then dance steps 17–22.

JIVE

Flicks into Break

Entry. Whip or Rock Basic.

Step	Feet Positions	Amount of Turn	Timing
Gentleman			
1–2	Dance two steps of Basic in "Fallaway" L, R	¼ to L	1, 2
3	LF forward leaning forward	None	3, 4
4	RF forward leaning back	None	1, 2
5	LF forward leaning forward	None	3, 4
6	Flick RF forward (still in PP)	None	1
7	RF side turning R to face partner	¼ to R	2
8	Flick LF forward in CPP	¼ to R	3
9	LF to side turning L to face partner	¼ to L	4
10–13	Repeat steps 6–9		1, 2, 3, 4
14	RF forward flat in front of LF in PP	¼ to L	1, 2 ,3 (¾)
15	Transfer weight sharply to LF	None	a (¼)

Step	Feet Positions	Amount of Turn	Timing
16	Transfer weight sharply to RF	None	4
F	Follow with Jive Chassés L, R, L, R, L, R, or "Fallaway" Throwaway.	None	

Lady

Step	Feet Positions	Amount of Turn	Timing
1–2	Dance two steps of Basic in "Fallaway" R, L	$\frac{1}{4}$ to R	1, 2
3	RF forward leaning forward	None	3, 4
4	LF forward leaning back	None	1, 2
5	RF forward leaning forward	None	3, 4
6	Flick LF forward (still in PP)	None	1
7	LF to side turning L to face partner	$\frac{1}{4}$ to L	2
8	Flick RF forward in CPP	$\frac{1}{4}$ to L	3
9	RF to side turning R to face partner	$\frac{1}{4}$ to R	4
10–13	Repeat steps 6–9		1, 2, 3, 4
14	LF forward in front of RF in PP	$\frac{1}{4}$ to R	1, 2, 3 ($\frac{3}{4}$)
15	Transfer weight sharply to RF	None	a ($\frac{1}{4}$)
16	Transfer weight sharply to LF	None	4

Footwork. Ball flat on each step except step 15 which is ball.

Exits. Rock Basic or Change of Places right to left.

Ending to Stop and Go

Entry. The first 5 steps of Stop and Go are described on page 128.

Step	Feet Positions	Amount of Turn	Timing
Gentleman			
1	RF forward	None	1
2	Replace weight on LF raising lady's arm	None	2
3	Very short step forward RF turning lady to her R	None	3
4	Very short step forward LF still turning lady to her R	None	4
5, 6, 7	Dance Jive Chassé R, L, R turning lady sharply to her R	None	3 a 4
Lady			
1	LF back	None	1
2	Replace weight on RF	(a full turn is made to R between steps 2, 3, 4)	2
3	LF to side and slightly back		3
4	RF side and slightly back		4
5, 6, 7	Dance a Jive Chassé L, R, L	Turning approx $1\frac{1}{2}$ turns to R between steps 5, 6, 7	3 a 4

Exit. Change of Places L to R.

Note. Rolling off the arm can also be danced after Stop and Go.

Toe Heel Swivels

Step	Feet Positions	Amount of Turn	Timing
Gentleman			
Entry. Precede with "Fallaway" Throwaway or Change of Places L to R taking Lady's L hand in R hand, still holding her R hand in L hand			1, 2, 3 a 4 3 a 4
1	Bring L toe to R toe without weight, toe turned in, swivelling to R on R foot	$\frac{1}{8}$ to R	1
2	Place L heel to side without weight, toe turned out, swivelling to L on RF	$\frac{1}{8}$ to L	2
3	Cross LF over in front of RF swivelling to R on RF	$\frac{1}{8}$ to R	3
4	Bring R toe to L toe without weight, toe turned in, swivelling to L on LF	$\frac{1}{8}$ to L	4
5	Place R heel to side without weight, toe turned out, swivelling to R on LF	$\frac{1}{8}$ to R	1
6	Cross RF over in front of LF, swivelling to L on LF	$\frac{1}{8}$ to L	2
7–8	Repeat 1, 2		3, 4

STANDARDIZED VARIATIONS

Step	Feet Positions	Amount of Turn	Timing
9–14	Exit two Jive Chassés L, R, L, R, L, R, taking normal hold		3 a 4 3 a 4

Lady

Step	Feet Positions	Amount of Turn	Timing
1	Bring R toe to L toe without weight, toe turned in, swivelling to L on LF	$\frac{1}{8}$ to L	1
2	Place R heel to side without weight, toe turned out, swivelling to R on LF	$\frac{1}{8}$ to R	2
3	Cross RF over in front of LF, swivelling to L on LF	$\frac{1}{8}$ to L	3
4	Bring L toe to R toe without weight, toe turned in, swivelling to R on RF	$\frac{1}{8}$ to R	4
5	Place L heel to side without weight, toe turned out, swivelling to L on RF	$\frac{1}{8}$ to L	1
6	Cross LF over in front of RF, swivelling to R on RF	$\frac{1}{8}$ to R	2
7–8	Repeat 1, 2		3, 4

Exits. Rock Basics or Change of Places R to L.

CHA CHA CHA
The Fall Over Step (Cuban Break)
Entry. Basic Movement (backward half).

Step	Feet Positions	Amount of Turn	Timing
1	LF forward (short step), turning slightly to R	⅛ to R	2 or Q
2	Replace weight on RF turning slightly to L	⅛ to L	and Q
3	LF to side	None	3 or Q
4	Replace weight on RF	None	and or Q
5	LF forward (short step) turning slightly to R	⅛ to R	4 or Q
6	Replace weight on RF turning slightly to L	⅛ to L	and or Q
7	LF to side	None	1 or S

Exit. Time step

Footwork. Ball flat on each step.

Note. This figure can be danced by the lady or gentleman simultaneously on opposite feet, or the lady can dance the Time Step while the gentleman dances the Fall Over, or vice versa.

The Original Follow My Leader
Gentleman

Entry. Ten steps Natural Top R, L, R, L, R, L, R, L, R, L. Count 2, 3, 4, and 1, 2, 3, 4 and 1. He then releases his partner.

1	RF forward	Commencing to turn to R	2
2	LF forward	Still turning R to complete ½ turn to R	3
3–5	Cha Cha Cha Chassé R, L, R,		4 and 1

STANDARDIZED VARIATIONS

Step	Feet Positions	Amount of Turn	Timing
	travelling slightly forward		
6	LF forward	Commencing to turn to L	2
7	RF forward	Still turning L to complete ½ turn to L	3
8–10	Cha Cha Cha Chassé L, R, L, travelling slightly forward		4 and 1
11–20	Repeat these ten steps		2, 3, 4 and 1
			2, 3, 4 and 1
21	RF back	None	2
22	Replace weight on LF	None	3
23–25	Cha Cha Cha Chassé R, L, R	None	4 a 1

Note. Gentleman releases lady after dancing the top.

Lady

Entry. Ten steps Natural Top. L, R, L, R, L, R, L, R, L, R. Count 2, 3, 4 and 1, 2, 3, 4 and 1.

Step	Feet Positions	Amount of Turn	Timing
1	LF back	None	2
2	Replace weight on RF	None	3
3–5	Cha Cha Cha Chassé L, R, L	None	4 and 1
6	RF forward	Commencing to turn to L	2
7	LF forward	Still turning L to complete ½ turn to L	3
8–10	Cha Cha Cha Chassé R, L, R, travelling slightly forward	None	4 and 1

Step	Feet Positions	Amount of Turn	Timing
11	LF forward	Commencing to turn to R	2
12	RF forward	Still turning to R to complete ½ turn to R	3
13–15	Cha Cha Cha Chassé L, R, L, travelling slightly forward		4 and 1
16–25	Repeat steps 6–15		2, 3, 4 and 1 2, 3, 4 and 1

Footwork. Ball flat on each step.

Note. When dancing steps 1–5 the gentleman can release lady with his R hand and turn her 1 complete turn to R. He then releases her with his hand.

The Sweetheart

Entry. Commence in Fan Position and lead lady into the Hockey Stick, changing R hand to R hand on count of the last 4 and 1.

Gentleman

1–5	Dance forward half of Basic Movement, LF, RF, LF, RF, LF, leading lady to step back RF, forward LF, forward RF, and leading her to complete a Cha Cha Cha Chassé, turning her ½ turn to her L to finish on gentleman's R side, both facing the same way. He will take her L hand in his L hand as she completes the turn, now holding both hands with a high hold	2, 3, 4 and 1
6	Forward RF leading lady to step back with LF	2
7	Replace on to LF (lady RF)	3
8–10	Cha Cha Cha Chassé to R passing lady in front to L side. She dancing Cha Cha Cha Chassé to L	4 and 1

STANDARDIZED VARIATIONS

Step	Feet Positions	Timing
11	Forward LF leading lady to step back with RF	2
12	Replace on to RF (lady LF)	3
13–15	Cha Cha Cha Chassé to L passing lady in front to R side. She dancing Cha Cha Cha Chassé to R	4 and 1
16	RF back leading lady to step back on LF	2
17	Replace weight on to LF (lady RF)	3
18–20	Both dance Cha Cha Cha Chassés moving forward and passing foot with slight "run" action	4 and 1
21	Forward LF with slight checking action leading lady to step forward RF	2
22	Replace weight on to RF (lady LF)	3
23–25	Both dance Cha Cha Cha Chassés moving backwards passing feet with slight running action	4 and 1
26	RF back leading lady to step back LF	2
27	Replace weight on to LF (lady RF)	3
28–30	Both dance Cha Cha Cha Chassés, gentleman moving to R and lady to L. He releases her hands and then takes lady's R hand in his L hand. Finish in fan position	4 and 1

Footwork. Ball flat on each step.

Exit. As for Fan.

Turkish Towel

Preceded by the Hockey Stick finishing with the lady's R hand in his R hand.

Step	Feet Positions	Timing
1	LF forward (lady RF back)	2
2	Replace weight on RF (lady LF)	3
3–5	Cha Cha Cha Chassé LF, RF, LF, moving slightly to L, lady RF, LF, RF, moving forward	4 and 1

Step	Feet Positions	Amount of Turn	Timing
6	RF back, raising R arms, turning lady on LF ½ turn to her R		2
7	Replace weight on LF turning lady a further ½ turn to R on her RF		3
8–10	A Cha Cha Cha Chassé RF, LF, RF moving slightly to R and leading lady behind his back to dance a Cha Cha Cha Chassé LF, RF, LF, curving ½ turn to R to finish on his L side. He now has her L hand in his L hand and her R hand in his R hand		4 and 1
11	LF back leading lady RF forward with his L hand		2
12	Replace weight on RF lady on LF		
13–15	Cha Cha Cha Chassé L, R, L, travelling very slightly to L and leading lady behind his back to dance a Chassé R, L, R, to finish on his R side		4 and 1
16	RF back leading lady LF forward with his R hand		2
17	Replace weight on LF, lady on RF		3
18–20	Repeat steps 8–10		4 and 1
21–25	Repeat steps 11–15 but on step 25 the man leads the lady to commence to turn to L with his R hand, he releases her and she continues to turn		2, 3, 4 and 1

Footwork. Ball flat on each step.

Exit. Gentleman dances second half of basic movement but turning very slightly to R, R, L, R, L, R, 2, 3, 4 and 1.

Lady continues to turn to L, L, R, L, R, L, 2, 3, 4 and 1 completing just under 1½ turns to L.

Rope Spinning

This is as described on page 24, except that on steps 3 and 6 a Cha Cha Cha Chassé is danced, timing 4 and 1.

4 3 2 1

5

6
 a chassis
7   fall away.

8

9